Battlefield
of the
mind

DEVOTIONAL

Battlefield
of the
mind

DEVOTIONAL

100 Insights That Will Change the Way You Think

JOYCE MEYER

New York   Boston   Nashville

Unless otherwise indicated, all Scripture quotations are taken from THE AMPLIFIED BIBLE: Old Testament. Copyright © 1962, 1964 by Zondervan Publishing House (used by permission); and from THE AMPLIFIED NEW TESTAMENT. Copyright © 1958 by the Lockman Foundation (used by permission).

All Scripture quotations noted CEV are taken from THE CONTEMPORARY ENGLISH VERSION. © 1991 by the American Bible Society. Used by permission.

All Scripture quotations noted The Message are taken from *The Message: The New Testament in Contemporary English.* Copyright © 1993 by Eugene H. Peterson.

All Scripture quotations noted NKJV are taken from THE NEW KING JAMES VERSION. Copyright © 1979, 1980, 1982, Thomas Nelson, Inc., Publishers.

All Scripture quotations noted KJV are taken from the King James Version of the Bible.

The Scripture quotation on page 91 is taken from THE LIVING BIBLE. Copyright © 1971, Tyndale House Publishers Inc.

Warner Faith
Time Warner Book Group
1271 Avenue of the Americas, New York, NY 10020

Visit our Web site at www.warnerfaith.com

The Warner Faith name and logo are registered trademarks of the Time Warner Book Group.
Printed in the United States of America

First Warner Books printing: October 2005

10 9 8 7 6 5 4 3 2

ISBN: 0-446-57706-5

LCCN: 2005929371

CONTENTS

1	The Invitation	1
2	Well-Laid Plans	4
3	Satan's Strongholds	8
4	The Devil's Lies	11
5	Know the Truth	15
6	Undercurrents	18
7	The Blame Game	22
8	As We Focus	26
9	Power of the Spirit	30
10	Known by Our Fruit	33
11	Don't Quit!	36
12	"I Can't Help It!"	40
13	Wilderness Mentality	44
14	Little by Little	47
15	First the Suffering	50
16	No Condemnation	54
17	No Hope	57
18	My Feelings	60
19	Positive Minds	63
20	A Perfect Plan	66

21	All Things Work for Good	69
22	Getting What We Want	72
23	No More Excuses	76
24	Why This Negativity?	79
25	Ready Minds	83
26	Positive Belief	87
27	The Waiting God	91
28	Evil Forebodings	94
29	Hold Your Tongue	98
30	Mind-Binding Spirits	101
31	Decide to Believe	105
32	Be Careful What You Think	109
33	Meditation Produces Success	112
34	"I Want a Mind Change"	116
35	A Transformed Mind	120
36	Think About What You Are Thinking About	123
37	The Condition of Our Minds	126
38	My Normal Mind	129
39	Still, Small Voice	133
40	Spiritual Praying	136
41	God's Vision for You	140
42	The Peaceful Mind	143
43	A Wandering, Wondering Mind	146
44	A Wondering Mind	149
45	A Confused Mind	153
46	Just Obey	157
47	Doing the Word	161
48	Trust God	164

49	Nothing But Christ	168
50	A Doubtful Mind	171
51	The Sin of Unbelief	174
52	Defeating Unbelief	177
53	Keep Walking on the Water!	180
54	Time to Worship	183
55	Why the Storms?	186
56	Doubt Is a Choice	189
57	A Tempting Offer	192
58	The Disobedience of Unbelief	195
59	A Sabbath Rest	199
60	From Faith to Faith	203
61	Don't Let the Devil Steal It	207
62	Anxious Minds	210
63	Greater Things	214
64	Reminders	217
65	Our Responsibility—God's Responsibility	221
66	Right from the Heart	225
67	Seek God, Not Gifts	228
68	D.V.	231
69	Casting Our Cares Upon God	234
70	Holy Fear	238
71	Wasted Life	241
72	Real Problems	245
73	The Critical Mind	249
74	"I" Problems	252
75	When Someone Fails	255
76	Passing Judgment	259

77	Loving One Another	262
78	Guarding Our Hearts	265
79	Suspicious of Suspicion	268
80	Trust God Completely	271
81	Pleasant Words, Healing Words	275
82	Passive Minds	278
83	Overcoming Passivity	282
84	Right Action Follows Right Thinking	285
85	The Mind of Christ	288
86	Go with God's Flow	291
87	Fear Not!	295
88	Be Thankful—Always	298
89	Tips for Being Thankful	301
90	Meditate on These Things	304
91	The Blessings of Meditation	307
92	Anointed to Bring Deliverance	310
93	Eyes to See, Ears to Hear	313
94	What's the Problem?	316
95	Bad Input Produces Bad Results	319
96	Responsibility?	322
97	Timing Is Everything	325
98	Instant Gratification	328
99	Too Hard?	331
100	Truth in the Inner Being	335

1

The Invitation

What I have forgiven . . . has been for your sakes . . . to keep Satan from getting the advantage over us; for we are not ignorant of his wiles and intentions.

—2 Corinthians 2:10–11

Suppose we receive a package from an overnight carrier. After we open it, we stare at a beautiful, oversized envelope, with our name written on it in exquisite calligraphy. Inside, the invitation starts with these words:

You are invited to enjoy a life filled with misery, worry, and confusion.

Which one of us would say yes to such an outrageous invitation? Don't we seek the kind of life that keeps us free from such pain and distractions? Yet many of us choose such a life. Not that we blatantly make that choice, but we sometimes surrender—even temporarily—to Satan's invitation. His attack is ongoing and relentless—the devil is persistent! Our enemy bombards our minds with every weapon at his disposal every day of our lives.

We are engaged in a warfare—a warfare that rages and never stops. We can put on the whole armor of God, halt the evil one's advances, and stand fast on the Word of God, but we won't put a complete end to the war. As long as we are alive, our minds remain Satan's battlefield. Most of our problems are rooted in thinking patterns that produce the problems we experience. This is where Satan triumphs—he offers wrong thinking to all of us. This isn't a new trick devised for our generation; he began his deceptive ways in the Garden of Eden. The serpent asked the woman, "Can it really be that God has said, You shall not eat from every tree of the garden?" (Genesis 3:1a). That was the first attack on the human mind. Eve could have rebuked the tempter; instead, she told him God would let them eat from the trees, but not from one particular tree. They couldn't even touch that tree, because if they did, they would die.

"But the serpent said to the woman, You shall not surely die, For God knows that in the day you eat of it your eyes will be opened, and you will be like God, knowing the difference between good and evil and blessing and calamity" (vs. 4–5).

This was the first attack, and it resulted in Satan's first victory. What we often miss about temptation and the battle our enemy levels against us is that it comes to us deceptively. Suppose he had said to the woman, "Eat of the fruit. You'll bring misery, anger, hatred, bloodshed, poverty, and injustice into the world."

Eve would have recoiled and run away. He tricked her because he lied and told her what would appeal to her.

Satan promised, "You will be like God. You'll know good and evil." What a marvelous appeal to the woman. He wasn't tempting Eve to do something bad—or at least he phrased it in such a way that what she heard sounded good.

That's always the appeal of sin or satanic enticement. The temptation is not to do evil or to cause harm or bring injustice. The lure is that we will gain something.

Satan's temptation worked on Eve. "And when the woman saw that the tree was good (suitable, pleasant) for food and that it was delightful to look at, and a tree to be desired in order to make one wise, she took of its fruit and ate; and she gave some also to her husband, and he ate" (3:6).

Eve lost the first battle for the mind, and we have continued to fight for it since that time. But because we have the power of the Holy Spirit in our lives, we can win—and we can keep on winning.

———————

Victorious God, help me resist the onslaughts of Satan, who attacks my mind and makes evil seem good. I ask this in the name of Jesus Christ. Amen.

2

Well-Laid Plans

For we are not wrestling with flesh and blood [contending only with physical opponents], but against the despotisms, against the powers, against [the master spirits who are] the world rulers of this present darkness, against the spirit forces of wickedness in the heavenly (supernatural) sphere.
—Ephesians 6:12

"How could you?" Helen screamed. "How could you ever do such a thing?"

Tom stared helplessly at his wife. He had committed adultery, faced his sinful actions, and asked his wife to forgive him.

"But you knew it was wrong," she said. "You knew that was the ultimate betrayal of our marriage."

"I never planned for an affair to happen," Tom said with tears in his eyes.

Tom wasn't lying. He knew he was making a few bad choices, but he hadn't looked ahead at the consequences of his actions. After almost an hour of pleading, he said something that helped Helen begin to understand and eventually to forgive.

"I was unfaithful to you in hundreds of ways before I ever committed adultery." He spoke of their being too busy to spend quality time together, his critical attitude, her occasional lack of emotional response, her not listening to him when he talked about problems at the office. "Just little things, always little things," he said. "At least in the beginning they seemed that way."

That's exactly how Satan works in human lives. He begins by bombarding our minds with cleverly devised patterns of irritation, dissatisfaction, nagging thoughts, doubts, fears, and reasonings. He moves slowly and cautiously (after all, well-laid plans take time).

Tom said he began to doubt that Helen truly loved him. She didn't listen, and she didn't always respond to his amorous moods. He dwelt on those thoughts. Whenever she did anything he didn't like, he kept track. He kept track by remembering and adding that to his list of dissatisfactions.

One of his coworkers listened, and she offered him sympathy. One time she said, "Helen doesn't deserve a warm, caring man like you." (Satan also worked in her.) Each time Tom took a tiny step off the right path, he justified his actions in his mind: *If Helen won't listen to me, there are people who will.* Although he said the word *people* to himself, he really meant the woman in the next cubicle.

The coworker listened. Weeks later, he hugged her and as he did so, he wished he could feel that caring response from his wife. It was a harmless embrace—or so it seemed. Tom didn't grasp that Satan is never in a hurry. He takes time to work out his plans. He doesn't immediately overwhelm people with powerful desires. Instead, the enemy of our minds starts with little things—little dissatisfactions, small desires—and builds from there.

Tom's story sounds much like that of a forty-two-year-old bookkeeper who was indicted for stealing nearly three million dollars from her organization. She said, "The first time I took only twelve dollars. I needed that much to pay the minimum amount on my credit card. I planned to pay it back." No one caught her, and two months later, she "borrowed" again.

By the time they caught her, the company teetered on the brink of bankruptcy. "I never meant to hurt anybody or do anything wrong," she said. She never intended to do anything big—just to take small amounts. The prosecutor said she had been stealing from the company for almost twenty years.

That's how Satan works—slowly, diligently, and in small ways. Rarely does he approach us through direct assault or frontal attacks. All Satan needs is an opening—an opportunity to inject unholy, self-centered thoughts into our heads. If we don't kick them back out, they stay inside. And he can continue his evil, destructive plan.

We don't have to allow those wrong thoughts to take up residence in our heads. The apostle Paul wrote, "For the weapons of our warfare are . . . mighty before God. . . . [We] refute arguments and theories and reasonings and every proud and lofty thing that sets itself up against the [true] knowledge of God; and we lead every thought and purpose away captive into the obedience of Christ . . ." (2 Corinthians 10:4–5).

———————

Lord Jesus, in Your name, I cry out for victory. Enable me to bring every thought into obedience. Help me not to allow Satan's words to stay in my mind and steal my victory. Amen.

3

Satan's Strongholds

For the weapons of our warfare are not physical [weapons of flesh and blood], but they are mighty before God for the overthrow and destruction of strongholds.

—2 CORINTHIANS 10:4

A stronghold is an area in which we are held in bondage—any part of our lives in which Satan imprisons us. He does this by causing us to think a certain way—a way that is based on lies we have been told. As long as we believe things that are not true, we will remain imprisoned by those strongholds. To enjoy freedom, we must learn to use God's mighty weapons.

In my book *Battlefield of the Mind,* I referred to Mary, who had been mistreated and brainwashed by her father, and by the time she was a teen, she didn't trust men. It's no wonder that she and her husband faced many conflicts in their marriage. For years, Satan had lied to her and she believed the lies.

Mary isn't one isolated case. I know a man named Daniel, who is quite intelligent. In fact, his family used to tell him he was the smartest man in town. God had given him a good mind, but Satan used that fact to imprison him. Until he met Jesus Christ, Daniel believed he was smarter than and superior to everyone else. Because of his pride, it was easy for him to be deceived and think more highly of himself than he should. He became critical and judgmental of others who he felt were not as brilliant as he believed he was.

Patricia was somewhat like Mary, except that her father constantly told her she was no good; that she was worthless and should marry the first man who would have her. That's exactly what she did, and she lived a miserable life. She felt she was never good enough for anyone.

Mary, Daniel, and Patricia had been trapped in different prisons, but Satan was the jail keeper. All three lived miserable lives until they leaned what Paul meant by "the weapons of our warfare." The Word of God is the weapon that set them free. That weapon became effective through preaching, teaching, books, tapes, seminars, small Bible study groups, and their own private studies. They also learned to turn to other spiritual weapons such as praise and prayer. They learned that when we genuinely praise God from our hearts, we defeat the devil quicker than by using any other battle plan.

They didn't overcome every problem the first day—it was a slow process, but it was worth the wait. Patricia later said, "It took a lot of years for me to become imprisoned through the lies of Satan, so why not give God plenty of time to work His good plan into my life?" Our victory is not a one-time, big event—it is a process.

"The more I realized how badly Satan played with my mind," Daniel said, "the more I could stand against him. The truth of God's Word made me free."

Praise and prayer are great weapons that God's people should use in overcoming the power of the evil one. Praise helps us keep our minds on God, His power, and the good things that are taking place in our lives. It is proof that we believe He can and will help us.

True prayer reflects a relationship with God and shows that we depend on Him. We are His children, and He is our Father. When we pray, we open the door for God's help. We ask Him to free our minds and give us victory over Satan's strongholds.

God answers those prayers. In fact, God is more eager to answer our prayers for help than we are to ask. Think of prayer this way: when we pray in faith, tremendous power is made available to us.

As we truly understand that we are God's children, we will gain confidence to use the weapons of our warfare. The weapons are there. We just need instruction on how to use them and encouragement not to give up. Jesus has promised to be with us always (see Matthew 28:20). We can win with our weapons because they are *spiritual* weapons. The devil fights a carnal, fleshly warfare, but we can win because we have the power of God on our side.

Precious Holy Spirit, teach me to understand that the weapons of our warfare are spiritual and that we can win against every attack of the devil. In Christ's name, I pray. Amen.

4

The Devil's Lies

[Jesus said]
You are of your father, the devil, and it is your will to practice
the lusts and gratify the desires [which are characteristic] of
your father. He was a murderer from the beginning and does
not stand in the truth, because there is no truth in him. When
he speaks a falsehood, he speaks what is natural to him, for
he is a liar [himself] and the father of lies and of all that is
false.

—John 8:44

The devil lies. In fact, the devil doesn't know how to speak the truth.

Most Christians know that—and yet they still listen to his evil words. Sometimes the lies seem to just pop into our minds for no apparent reason; sometimes Satan even speaks to us through other people. He puts something critical or hurtful into their minds about us, and they speak it out for us to hear. If we listen and accept what we hear, our enemy rejoices. If we listen long enough to the deceptive information we have taken in, we will find ourselves facing serious problems. Instead of listening and absorbing the untruths and satanic deceptions, you can look at what Jesus did and follow His example. After fasting for forty days in the wilderness, Satan tempted Him three times. Each time He defeated the devil by declaring, "It is written," and quoting the Word of God. No wonder the devil fled from Him (see Matthew 4:1–11). Learn the truth of God's Word, and every time Satan lies to you, quote a scripture back to him. Learn to talk back to the devil!

Too many people don't know how to use the Word to defeat Satan's lies. Many people—even Christians—don't seem to realize that they can refuse to listen to that voice. Too many people don't realize that the devil attacks their minds with negative or wrong thoughts. It's his nature to lie; he is out to enslave everyone.

I encourage people to realize that they are not alone in their spiritual battles—their minds are not the only ones under attack. Satan comes against everyone. His entire goal is to kill, steal, and destroy, but Jesus came that we might have and enjoy our lives abundantly (see John 10:10). By becoming more conscious of the spiritual weapons the Lord has made available to us and learning how to use them, we can gain victory. We can break the strongholds the devil has built in our minds. The Bible tells us that when we know the truth, that truth will free us from Satan's strongholds (see John 8:32).

In the illustration of Mary, I mentioned that the devil had whispered to her for years that all men were alike and wanted to hurt women and take advantage of them. As Mary read the Bible and prayed more effectively, she learned that it was the devil who had pushed her around. Now she knows she can be free.

As Mary develops in her relationship with God, she is equipping herself to win the battle for her mind. She's learning more about God and more about how to pray effectively.

"Jesus has become my friend," Mary said. She had known Him as her Savior and worshiped Him as God, but this was a new revelation to her. One day she read Hebrews 2:18 in a totally new light. It says of Jesus, "Because He Himself [in His humanity] has suffered in being tempted (tested and tried), He is able . . . to run to the cry of (assist, relieve) those who are being tempted."

That passage came alive to Mary because she saw Jesus not only as God, but as her friend—one who knows what it's like to be tempted and who knows what it is like to suffer. "I knew He died on the cross, but I had not thought of all the pain He went through for me. To realize that He understands my pain and problems was a new thought to me."

Mary also says that when negative, mean, or ugly thoughts come into her head, she is learning to stop those thoughts. "Jesus wouldn't talk that way. Jesus wouldn't be critical and judgmental, so that's the devil fighting for my mind."

Mary hasn't won all the battles, but she has learned to fight the great deceiver. Every time she wins one battle, the next one becomes easier.

God of all power, thank You for giving me the weapons to defeat the lies of the devil. Help me to always make good use of them. Thank You, Jesus, for being my friend and for being with me in my difficulties and struggles. Amen.

5

Know the Truth

[Jesus said]
If you abide in My word [hold fast to My teachings and live in accordance with them], you are truly My disciples. And You will know the Truth, and the Truth will set you free.

—JOHN 8:31b–32

In my book *Battlefield of the Mind*, I also write about Mary's husband, John, a low-key type person. He was a man who had been verbally abused by his mother and taunted by playmates in childhood. He hated confrontation and couldn't stand up to Mary's strong will. In his own way, John was as much a prisoner as his wife. He blamed her; she blamed him—and here we see Satan's deceptive ways again.

John was convinced that it didn't do any good to stand up to anyone; he was going to lose anyway. He thought the only way to get along was to be quiet and accept whatever happened.

John also believed another lie of the devil—that he wasn't truly loved by God. How could he be? He wasn't worth loving. Because he felt that way, he had believed the devil's lies. "I felt as if God said to the world, 'Believe in Jesus and you'll be saved.' I got in on some kind of package deal—but I never felt I was worth loving."

That is one of Satan's biggest lies: "You are nobody. You are not worth anything." If the enemy of your mind can convince you that you're too bad or too worthless, he has set up a stronghold in your mind.

Although John was a Christian, his mind had been imprisoned by his enemy. John has had to learn that he is important to God. For a long time, he did not know the truth. His mother had not told him that he was good, worthwhile, and a child of God. His friends didn't encourage him, and in the first years of marriage to Mary, her criticism convinced him even further that he was a hopeless failure.

John needs to know that he is loved, and that he is as valuable to the kingdom of God as Paul, Moses, or anybody else. Jesus cares for him, and He is with him. For John to win his battle and cast down the mental strongholds the devil has built, he needs to know the truth. Jesus said, "If you . . . [hold fast to My teachings and live in accordance with them], you are truly My disciples. And you will know the Truth, and the Truth will set you free" (John 8:31b–32). John learns truth as he reads God's Word, prays, and meditates on what it says to him. He also learns as he applies God's Word in his daily life and has the experience of watching it work as Jesus said it would. Experience is often the best teacher. I have learned from the Word of God and life's experiences that God's Word is filled with power and will tear down the strongholds Satan has built in our minds.

You cannot be free unless you know that the weapons of warfare are available to you and that you can learn to use them. As you learn to resist Satan and call him a liar, your life will change dramatically for the better.

Lord God of heaven, remind me that I am important to You and that I am loved by You, even if I don't feel loved. Help me to learn that I am as important to You as any other Christian and that You love me as much as You love them. I thank You in the name of Jesus Christ. Amen.

6

Undercurrents

[Jesus said]
The Spirit of the Lord [is] upon Me, because He has anointed
Me [the Anointed one, the Messiah] to preach the good news
(the Gospel) to the poor; He has sent Me to announce release
to the captives and recovery of sight to the blind, to send forth
as delivered those who are oppressed [who are downtrodden,
bruised, crushed, and broken down by calamity], to proclaim
the accepted and acceptable year of the Lord [the day when
salvation and the free favors of God profusely abound.]
—LUKE 4:18–19

My husband, Dave, and I had been active in the church for a long time. At church, we had bright smiles and mixed well with other church members. I'm sure people thought we were the ideal couple.

But we weren't ideal. We had a strife-laden marriage—and it showed in the home. When we arrived at church, we set aside all the strife for a period of time. After all, we did not want our friends to know what things were really like at home behind closed doors.

Dave and I had constant strife—but strife isn't always open warfare. Strife is partially defined as an angry undercurrent.

We bickered and argued at times, but we also frequently pretended everything was fine between us. I look back now and believe that we didn't fully realize we had a problem. The Bible teaches us that we speak out of our hearts. If we had only really listened to what we said about and to one another, we would have realized that something was wrong. For example, we made jokes in public about each other. "She thinks she's the boss," Dave would say. "She wants what she wants and stays on me until she gets it. Joyce wants to control everything and everybody." Then he would pause to kiss me on top of my head and smile.

"I don't think Dave's hearing is very good," I'd say. "I nearly always have to ask him four times to take out the garbage." I'd smile, and everyone was supposed to know it was a joke.

Not everyone picked up on the undercurrents, but they were there. Those who frequently visited our home eventually saw even more chaos and underlying anger. But we smiled and said, "I'm only kidding," when we put the other one down, so how could there be any real problems?

When the home atmosphere is terrible, the devil loves it. Division is his goal, and unfortunately, he is frequently winning in that situation. He loves it when people pretend and no one in the family actually faces the problems. That's ideal for the powers of darkness. Satan would have kept on winning unless Dave and I had learned the dangers of strife and faced the truth about ourselves. We had to look at ourselves and admit how we had failed God and one another. We needed to acknowledge that our smiles and jokes only masked the pain.

If Dave and I were going to defeat the attacks of the devil, we had to make drastic changes. We had to fight the undercurrents and bring the darkness into the light.

This is the same message for all of us. We need to open ourselves to God's Word and see our failings and shortcomings. We need to be able to say, "I have been wrong."

Dave and I had both developed a bad habit—I'll say it even stronger—Satan had made inroads into our minds. We had been justifying our behavior and blaming each other for our problems. We needed to be shown the error of our ways, and thank God, He did show us.

We had to study God's Word extensively, and both of us had to be willing to humble ourselves in order for the atmosphere in our home to be changed from one of bickering, arguing, heated disagreement, and an angry undercurrent to one of peace and joy. The Holy Spirit worked with us, and we now enjoy peace. We respect each other and try to use good manners in private as well as in public.

We finally stopped listening to Satan's lies. We began to use the weapons of God's Word, praise, and prayer, and we have experienced great victory over the strongholds that once existed in our minds.

———————————

Lord Jesus, I'm so glad You came to deliver those who are oppressed. Thank You for helping me realize that my oppression comes from Satan . . . and for providing the weapons of your Word and prayer that I can use to break free from the devil's powerful clutches. I pray, Lord Jesus, that I will remain free both now and forever. Amen.

7

The Blame Game

No temptation (no trial regarded as enticing to sin), [no matter how it comes or where it leads] has overtaken you and laid hold on you that is not common to man [that is, no temptation or trial has come to you that is beyond human resistance and that is not adjusted and adapted and belonging to human experience, and such as man can bear]. But God is faithful [to His Word and to His compassionate nature], and He [can be trusted] not to let you be tempted and tried and assayed beyond your ability and strength of resistance and power to endure, but with the temptation He will [always] also provide the way out (the means of escape to a landing place), that you may be capable and strong and powerful to bear up under it patiently.

—1 Corinthians 10:13

Years ago, a comedian's favorite punch line was, "The devil made me do it." The audience roared. Why did people laugh so hard? Was it because they wanted it to be true? Did they want to absolve themselves of responsibility for their actions by pointing to an outside force?

It's always easy to blame someone else or outside forces for our actions. We hear people all the time who tell us, "My father never said a kind word to me." "My cousin abused me." "People in our neighborhood shunned me because I wore old and patched clothes." "I never had money when I was growing up, so now as soon as my paycheck comes, it's gone."

Those statements are probably true, and they may explain why we suffer. Those are terrible situations, and it's sad that people should have to go through such pain in their lives.

Yet we don't have the right to blame other people or circumstances for our behavior. We can't use them as an excuse to stay in bondage. Christ came to set us free. In the opening verse, Paul makes it clear that all of us have our own set of temptations, and for each of us, the circumstances may be different. But the promise God gives is the certainty of a way to escape, regardless of our circumstances. The escape is provided, but we must make use of it.

On the morning news, the reporter showed a restaurant that had caught on fire. One woman stood within sight of the back exit but she didn't move. She stood twenty feet away and screamed. A coworker rushed back inside and grabbed her. She fought him, but he finally managed to drag her out.

Isn't that sometimes how it works with God's people? We know the way of escape, but we seem paralyzed. Or we blame someone or something for our inability to move. Or we think, *Here it is again. I know I should learn how to deal with these situations, but I'll give in just as I've always given in. I'm too weak to deal with this right now.*

Our weakness is one of our greatest excuses. We may be weak, but God is strong, and He is willing to be our strength.

If we will trust Him and take the necessary steps of faith, He will help us break free from our bondages.

What we need to understand is that Satan takes our circumstances—no matter what they are—and uses them to build strongholds in our lives. He'll use whatever he can—our sense of weakness, our problems from childhood, or the wrong things we did when we were twelve years old. If the devil can darken our minds—make us think we can't possibly win—we've lost. We need to keep reminding ourselves that we serve a victorious God who has provided the spiritual weapons we need to tear down the devil's strongholds.

One more thing: When we give in to the temptation, aren't we subtly saying that God is not able to help us? We don't enjoy taking full responsibility for our actions—or, in many cases, our inaction—but we need to. We need to stop feeling sorry for ourselves, shifting blame, and ignoring situations. We need to believe the promise of God that declares He is faithful and will always deliver us in plenty of time. We don't need to live in fear, always feeling that our problems are too much for us to handle. We must have a "can-do" attitude. One that says, "I can do whatever I need to do whenever I need to do it." Sometimes we are even tempted to blame God for our troubles, but we must remember the words previously quoted: ". . . but God is faithful . . . and He [can be trusted] not to let you be tempted . . . beyond your ability and strength of resistance . . ."

That's God's promise, and He lays His reputation on the line with that promise. God never abandons us or leaves us helpless. We can be like the woman who screamed but wouldn't move. Or we can choose to say, "Look! There's the door of escape! Thanks for providing it!"

Our problems are personal and they are often internal. They involve our thoughts and our attitudes. The results—the outward behavior—flow from those thoughts and attitudes. If we keep our mind turned toward Jesus, and if we listen to His voice, we know there is an escape route for us—always.

Father God, forgive me for blaming You, my circumstances, or other people for my failures. You are the Way-Maker for me in every temptation. I'm going to trust You to tear down the devil's strongholds in my mind, in Jesus' name. Amen.

8

As We Focus

For as he thinks in his heart, so is he.
—PROVERBS 23:7 (NKJV)

Years ago, I learned an invaluable lesson: Whatever we focus on, we become. That simple statement taught me a great deal. Wherever we put our energies or our attention, those things will develop. Another way I like to say it is, "Where the mind goes, the man follows!"

If I begin to think about ice cream, I will soon find myself in my car pursuing ice cream. My thought will stir my desires and emotions, and I will make the decision to follow them.

If we focus only on the negative things in our lives, we become negative people. Everything, including our conversation, becomes negative. We soon lose our joy and live miserable lives—and it all started with our own thinking.

You might be experiencing some problems in life—not realizing that you are creating them yourself by what you're choosing to think about. I challenge you to think about what you're thinking about!

You might be discouraged and even depressed and wonder

what caused it. Yet if you will examine your thought life, you will find that you are feeding the negative emotions you are feeling. Negative thoughts are fuel for discouragement, depression, and many other unpleasant emotions.

We should choose our thoughts carefully. We can think about what is wrong with our lives or about what is right with them. We can think about what is wrong with all the people we are in relationship with or we can see the good and meditate on that. The Bible teaches us to always believe the best. When we do that, it makes our own lives happier and more peaceful.

I have a great life—and a loving husband and children. And I am privileged to be used by God to bless millions of people around the world through the wonderful ministry He has given me. But life isn't perfect, and if I had allowed the devil to fill my mind with negative thoughts—as he once did long ago—I would have been defeated.

I want to focus on God's grace and give thanks for all the good things in my life. I don't want to focus on what I don't have.

An old friend used to quote this saying: "As you wander on through life, brother, whatever be your goal, keep your eye upon the donut and not upon the hole." Too many people focus on what's not there and what's not right.

All of this is to say that our thoughts largely determine our destiny. Our thoughts also determine our happiness. Proverbs 23:7 is one of my favorite verses. Thoughts are powerful. They aren't just words that flow through our minds. So it is very important for us to decide what we will allow to rest inside our minds.

We must not forget that the mind is a battlefield. We must always remember that our adversary will use it in any way he possibly can to trap us.

I'm reminded of a man who came to one of our meetings. He wanted deliverance from viewing pornography. He said that one time he had seen something on the Internet after accidentally logging on to a site that was filled with explicitly sexual pictures. The next day he laughed about it to one of his coworkers. "Who wants to watch that stuff?" he asked.

The next night he was back at the site again. And many nights after that. He purchased sexual material and had it sent to his office. He kept his stash of pornography hidden from his family. "What's a little thing like that going to hurt?" he reasoned.

He confessed that the more he saw the images, the more he thought of women as objects—objects for his pleasure. One day his wife said, "I don't know what's happened to you, but you can either deal with your attitude or I'm leaving."

His life was rapidly going downhill before he asked for prayer. "I never thought just watching a couple of porno sites like that could be so addictive," he said.

To put it another way, we can't have a positive life and a negative mind. Our thoughts—our focus—is what determines where we end up.

Jesus, our friend and Savior, wants our minds to be filled

with positive, beautiful, and healthy thoughts. The more we focus on those things, the more readily we defeat Satan's attacks.

————————————

Dear patient and loving God, I ask You to forgive me for focusing my thoughts on things that are not pleasing to You. I pray that You will help me fill my mind with thoughts that are clean and pure and uplifting. In Jesus' name. Amen.

9

Power of the Spirit

*Not by might, nor by power, but by My Spirit . . . says the
Lord of hosts.*

—Zechariah 4:6b (nkjv)

"I'm a nobody," my friend Gary said, "and besides, God has
so many millions of people to look out for, and in comparison
with some of them, my problems seem so petty."

His words shocked me. Of course, God has millions to
care for—but He can care for all of them at the same time.

Gary missed something very important. God wants us to
ask for help—and to ask often. Look at it this way: If Satan
constantly attacks our minds, how else can we fortify ourselves? We fight back—but our major weapon is to cry out to
the Lord asking for His strength to become ours.

Too many times, we think we can do it ourselves. In some
instances, that may be true, but if we're going to win continually over the attacks against our minds, we must realize that
willpower alone won't work. What we need is the humility to
turn to the Holy Spirit and ask Him to strengthen us.

I realize that many people do not grasp how the Lord lovingly operates in their lives. Not only does God love us like a father, but He also has caring concern for every part of our lives. Our heavenly Father wants to intervene and help us, but He waits for an invitation to get involved. We issue that invitation and open the door for God's help through prayer. God's Word says, "You do not have, because you do not ask" (James 4:2 NKJV).

Perhaps we can think of it this way. God is watching us all the time, and He is aware of the temptations, struggles, and hardships we face—and we all face them. If we think we can do it by ourselves, God takes no action. But He remains ready to jump in and rescue us as soon as we cry out, asking for the power of the Holy Spirit to operate in our lives.

Our victory begins with right thinking. We have to be convinced that God cares, wants to act, and waits for us to cry out. When we cry out, we understand the words quoted previously, that it's not by force or power, but by God's Holy Spirit that victory comes.

For example, take the matter of personal fellowship—daily time spent in prayer and reading the Word. As Christians, we know this is what God wants and what we need if we're going to mature spiritually. At one time in my life, I tried to maintain spiritual self-discipline. I determined that I would pray and read my Bible every single day. I would do well for two or three days, and then something would interfere—sometimes my family or something at our church, but mostly little things that took my attention away from daily fellowship with my Lord.

One day, in desperation, I cried out, "Without Your help, I'll never be faithful in doing this." That's when the Holy Spirit came to me and gave me the self-discipline I needed. It was almost as if God watched me struggle and allowed me to become frustrated and angry with myself. But as soon as I sincerely asked for help, the Spirit came to my rescue. We are too independent, and we experience a lot of unnecessary frustration simply because we try to do things without God's help.

With the Spirit's help, I am learning—yes, still learning—that I can choose what I want to think about. I can choose my thoughts, and I need to do that carefully. Unless I'm in regular fellowship with Him, I won't know the difference between healthy thoughts and unhealthy ones. And if I don't know the difference, I provide the opportunity for Satan to sneak into my mind and torment me. Spend plenty of time studying God's Word, and you will quickly recognize each lie that Satan tries to plant in your mind.

Dear loving God, I want to think thoughts that honor You. I want to have a mind that's fully centered on You, and I know that can't happen unless I spend daily time with You. Help me, Holy Spirit; help me to be obedient and eager to be in constant fellowship with You. Amen.

10

Known by Our Fruit

[Jesus said]
Either make the tree sound (healthy and good), and its fruit
sound (healthy and good), or make the tree rotten (diseased
and bad), and its fruit rotten (diseased and bad); for the
tree is known and recognized and judged by its fruit. You
offspring of vipers! How can you speak good things when
you are evil (wicked)? For out of the fullness (the overflow,
the superabundance) of the heart the mouth speaks.

—MATTHEW 12:33–34

A woman I'll call Dorothy knew more about the church and every member and visitor than anyone else did. She was fairly well known as the church gossip.

"One thing about her," a friend said, "she's not prejudiced— she talks about everyone," and he laughed. He also added, "She'll probably get into heaven, but God may have to cut off her tongue first."

One day as I stood near the front door, I heard Dorothy telling several people about one of the deacons, "But it isn't up to me to judge him," she said. The venom poured from her mouth, and she went on to mention several others. Of course, she was critical of each one.

I listened to her and realized something. She was only speaking from what was already inside her heart. That's obvious, but I grasped something else. Dorothy was so critical of herself, so filled with disgust for herself, how could she speak well of others?

Too often people make promises that they'll speak better of others and gossip less. They really try, but nothing ever changes. This is because they are trying to change their words without changing their thoughts. That's a bad solution, because they start at the wrong end. What they need to do is look inward, asking, "What is going on inside of me?"

"For out of the fullness of the heart, the mouth speaks," Jesus said. As I considered those words, I felt a deep compassion for Dorothy. She had allowed Satan to fill her mind with critical, harsh thoughts. She didn't speak much about herself, but I'm sure she was totally critical of herself as well as other people, and when she spoke, the evil words came out of her mouth.

Jesus said that a tree is known by its fruit. The same is true of our lives. Everything begins with a thought. If we allow negative and unkind thoughts to fill our minds, they bear fruit. If we dwell on the bad, we produce bad fruit.

As we observe people, it's easy to see the fruit of their lives. They show either good fruit or bad. It's that simple. But the fruit is the result of what's going on inside. We can learn a lot about a person's character simply by listening to their conversation. The more loving our words and actions are toward others, the more loving and kind our thoughts will be.

If I believe God truly loves me, and if I enjoy fellowship with Him every day, I'm planting good seeds in my own heart. The more good seeds I plant, the more good fruit I produce. The more I think kind and loving thoughts, the more I see others as kind and loving.

"Out of the fullness of the heart, the mouth speaks." Kind or judgmental words don't just come to us—they come out of our mouths because we have nurtured them in our minds. The more we open ourselves to the Spirit's positive and loving thoughts, the more we pray, and the more we read God's Word, the more good fruit we produce on the inside—and that good fruit shows itself by the way we behave toward others.

———————

Dear loving and forgiving God, I ask You to forgive me for all the harsh things I've said about other people. Also, please forgive me for allowing harsh thoughts to fill my mind—about myself or about others. I know I can't make myself more loving, but You can. Please, help me focus on healthy, positive thoughts, for I pray this in the name of Jesus Christ. Amen.

11

Don't Quit!

And let us not lose heart and grow weary and faint in acting nobly and doing right, for in due time and at the appointed season we shall reap, if we do not loosen and relax our courage and faint.

—GALATIANS 6:9

"I've been a Christian for twenty-three years," Cheryl said. "I'm just not getting anywhere. I'm as weak as I was when I first accepted Christ as my Savior. I still fail. I just don't know if it's worth it." Tears streamed down her cheeks as she continued to talk about her failures. "By now I know all the right things to do, but I don't do them. Sometimes I deliberately do something mean-spirited or unkind. What kind of Christian am I?"

"Probably a growing Christian," I said.

A startled look appeared on Cheryl's face. "Growing? Did you hear—?"

"Yes, I heard. But if you weren't growing, you wouldn't lament your failures. You'd be satisfied about your spiritual level or tell yourself how good you are."

"But I'm so discouraged, and I fail God so many times."

I went on to tell Cheryl she was correct—that she had failed. All of us do at times. None of us is perfect. If we're not careful, we allow the devil to point to what we haven't accomplished and where we have been weak. When that happens, it's easy to feel bad or want to give up.

That's not the way of the Spirit. No matter how we mess up our lives, God doesn't give up on us. The Spirit constantly nudges us.

We can allow our thoughts to dwell on what we haven't done, why we ought to be more spiritual, or how spiritual we ought to be after all these years in our Christian faith. That's a trick of the devil—to make us think of our defects and shortcomings. If we focus on what we're not or what we haven't accomplished, we are allowing the devil to make advances on the battlefield of our minds.

The fact that my troubled friend was upset was a healthy sign, even though she didn't see it that way. With the Holy Spirit's help, she can push back the devil. She can regain the territory Satan has stolen from her.

Cheryl seemed to think that holy, victorious living came from one major victory after another. Yes, we do have times when we have great breakthroughs; however, most of our victories come slowly. They come little by little. It's as if we inch forward. Because we move slowly in our spiritual growth, we are often unaware of how far we have moved. If the devil can make us think that we must have one decisive spiritual victory after another or we're losers, he has gained an important stronghold.

My advice to Cheryl, and to all Christians who face those dark moments, is to listen to the words of the apostle Paul. He exhorted us not to grow weary, or as another translation says it, "not to lose heart." He's saying, "Don't quit. Keep fighting."

Life is a struggle, and the devil is determined to defeat and destroy us. We don't ever reach the place where we never have to fight. But it's not just our fight. Jesus is not only *with* us, but He is *for* us. He's at our side to strengthen us and to urge us onward.

My friend kept remembering the times she had failed, but I reminded her of the times she had succeeded. "You think the devil is in control, but that's not true. You have failed, but you have also succeeded. You have stood your ground and you have made progress."

"Don't quit. Don't give up." That's the message we need to hear. I think of the words of Isaiah: "Fear not, for I have redeemed you . . . ; I have called you by your name; you are Mine. When you pass through the waters, I will be with you, and through the rivers, they will not overwhelm you. When you walk through the fire, you will not be burned or scorched, nor will the flame kindle upon you" (Isaiah 43:1b–2).

This is God's promise. He doesn't promise to take us completely out of troubles or hardships, but He does promise to be with us as we go through them. "Fear not," He says. That's the message we need to ponder. We don't need to fear because God is with us. And when God is with us, what is there to worry about?

———————————

God, despite my failures, You are with me, encouraging me not to give up. Please help me to remember that, with Your help, I can win. In the name of Jesus, I pray. Amen.

12

"I Can't Help It!"

*I call heaven and earth to witness this day against you that
I have set before you life and death, the blessings and the
curses; therefore choose life, that you and your descendants
may live.*

—Deuteronomy 30:19

When God begins to deal with us about wrong behavior, it's
easy enough to say, "I can't help it," but it takes real courage
and faith to say, "I'm ready to take responsibility and get my
life straightened out."

Avoidance, which is not facing issues, is a major problem.
Wrong things don't go away just because we refuse to acknowledge them. We often stuff things. We hide from them,
and as long as we do, they have power over us. Issues buried
alive never die.

For many years, I refused to deal with the sexual abuse in
my childhood. My father had abused me, so I left home the
week I turned eighteen years old. I thought I was getting
away from the problem by leaving, but I didn't realize I had
the problem in my soul. It was in my thoughts, attitudes, and

words. It affected my actions and all of my relationships. I had buried my past and stuffed my stuff. We don't have to live in the past—in fact, we are encouraged by God's Word to forget it and let it go. However, that doesn't mean that we are free to ignore the results of it and pretend that we are not hurting when we are.

I had a lot of bad behavior and negative attitudes. I also had lots of excuses. I wasn't dealing with anything from the past; I was merely feeling sorry for myself and saying, "I can't help it. It's not my fault I was abused." And it wasn't my fault. But it was my responsibility to let God help me overcome all the bondages I was experiencing as a result of that abuse.

God began setting me free by dealing with me about all the wrong thoughts I had accepted and allowed. My mind had to change before my life could change. At first, I didn't even want to take responsibility for my thoughts. I thought, *I can't help what I think—things just come into my head!* I eventually learned that I could choose my own thoughts, and I could think things on purpose. I learned that we don't have to accept every thought that falls into our minds. We can cast down wrong ones and replace them with right ones.

I learned that instead of feeling helpless over the thoughts that fill my mind, I can—I must—do something positive.

Much of our thinking is habitual. If we regularly think about God and good things, godly thoughts become natural. Thousands of thoughts flow through our minds every day. We may feel that we have no control, but we do. Although we don't have to use any effort to think wrong thoughts, we have to use much effort to think good thoughts. As we begin to make changes, we will have to fight a battle.

Our mind is the battlefield, and Satan's primary way of initiating his evil plan for us is through our thoughts. If we feel we have no power over our thoughts, Satan will entrap and defeat us. Instead, we can determine to think in godly ways. We constantly make choices. Where do those choices come from? They originate in our thought life. Our thoughts become our words and our actions.

God has given us the power to decide—to choose right thinking over wrong. But once we make that choice, we must continue to choose right thoughts. It's not a once-and-for-all decision, but it does get easier. The more we fill our lives with reading the Bible, prayer, praise, and fellowship with other believers, the easier it is for us to continue choosing right thoughts.

It may sound as if I'm saying that trying to live the Christian life is nothing but one continuous struggle. That's partly true, but that's only a piece of the story. Too many people want to live victorious Christian lives, but they don't want to fight the battles. Victory, however, means winning and overcoming obstacles. We must also remember that living a life of disobedience to God is harder than choosing to live in victory. Yes, there are struggles but they are worth it in the end.

To think in the right way takes practice, and it is not always easy, nor does it feel natural for us to focus only on the good. But if we know this is the pathway to life—both now and in eternity—it's worth the effort and the struggle to think positive thoughts.

When we're bombarded with doubts and fears, that's when we need to take our stand. We don't ever want to say again, "I can't help it." We want to believe and say, "God is with me, and He strengthens me. God enables me to win." The apostle Paul said it this way, "But thanks be to God, Who gives us the victory [making us conquerors] through our Lord Jesus Christ. Therefore, my beloved brethren, be firm (steadfast), immovable, always abounding in the work of the Lord [always being superior, excelling, doing more than enough in the service of the Lord], knowing and being continually aware that your labor in the Lord is not futile [it is never wasted or to no purpose]" (1 Corinthians 15:57–58).

We can choose. Not only can we choose, but we do choose. By not pushing the bad thoughts from our minds, we're allowing them to invade us and take us captive.

It takes time to learn to choose good and push away evil. It won't be easy, but we're moving in the right direction every time we take responsibility and make right choices.

Powerful God, remind me that I can and do make choices every day. Please help me to monitor my thoughts, choosing only those that will help me overcome the devil and win the battle for my mind. In Jesus name, I pray. Amen.

13

Wilderness Mentality

The Lord our God said to us in Horeb, You have dwelt long enough on this mountain. Turn and take up your journey and go to the hill country of the Amorites. . . . Behold, I have set the land before you; go in and take possession of the land which the Lord swore to your fathers, to Abraham, to Isaac, and to Jacob, to give to them and to their descendants after them.

—Deuteronomy 1:6–8

Those of us who are parents know these words so well: "In a minute. Just a little longer." We call our children to leave their playing and come inside, but they want just a little more time to stay out with their friends. For now, at least, they're content playing and don't want to think about getting cleaned up or eating dinner. It's always, "Just a little longer"—if we let them. And at times, we adults act a little like those children who cry out, "Just a little longer."

I've met miserable people—those who disliked their lives, hated their jobs, or were in intolerable relationships with the wrong kind of people. They knew they were miserable, but they did nothing about it. "Just a little longer." A little longer for what? More pain? More discouragement? More unhappiness?

Those are the people who have what I call the wilderness mentality. I want to explain that. Moses led the people of Israel out of Egypt. If they had obeyed God, stopped their grumbling, and moved straight ahead as God originally told them, they could have made the trip in eleven days. But it took them forty years.

Why did they finally leave? Only because God said, "You have dwelt long enough on this mountain." If God hadn't pushed them into the Promised Land, I wonder how long they would have stayed and longed to cross the Jordan.

They were people in bondage. Although they had seen miracles in Egypt and had praised God at the defeat of the Egyptian armies at the Red Sea, they were still in bondage. The chains were no longer on their bodies, but they had never removed those chains from their minds. That is the wilderness mentally.

For forty years, they grumbled. They had no water, and then God provided it for them. They grumbled about the food. Manna was all right, but they wanted meat of some kind. No matter what the situation, they were still mental prisoners. As they had been in Egypt, so they were in the wilderness. No matter how good things became, they were never good enough. They had forgotten all the hardships and slavery in Egypt, and every time they were dissatisfied with Moses' leadership they moaned, "Oh, if only we had stayed in Egypt."

They had forgotten how bad things were; they had no vision for how good things could get. When they had the chance to move into the new land, they were afraid. "There are giants in the land," they cried out. They had seen God's deliverance in the past, but they weren't ready for it in the present.

Finally God said, "Okay, it's time to move out." The Bible doesn't tell us about their attitude, but there's no reason to believe it had changed. I can imagine they cried out, "Let's stay just a little longer. Things aren't good here, but we know how to live in the wilderness. We are afraid to leave this place—we have become used to it."

If you don't like your life, but you won't make the effort to change, you may have a wilderness mentality. If your mind stays filled with negative thoughts, they will keep you in bondage.

However, you can do something about it. You don't have to waste any more time. You can say, "I've dwelt long enough at this mountain. Now I'm going into the Promised Land—the land where I'll live in victory and defeat Satan's plans."

Great God, help me cast off the wilderness mentality. Help me take on the Promised-Land mentality and live in victory, through Jesus Christ. Amen.

14

Little by Little

And the Lord your God will clear out those nations before you, little by little; you may not consume them quickly, lest the beasts of the field increase among you.
—DEUTERONOMY 7:22

Recently I thought about my life from the time I seriously began to follow Jesus Christ to the present. Had I known then—at the beginning of the journey—all the things God would take me through, I would probably have been afraid to sign up for the trip.

As I look back, however, I realize that God held my hand and let me advance in small steps. I had times of great discouragement—as we all do. I remember times of bitter tears over my personal failures. But God kept nudging me forward.

That's the secret of living the victorious Christian life—we move ahead little by little. It's an inching forward over months and years. Most of us can understand that. The same is true in the battle for the mind. We don't roust Satan in one big blow and then live in victory forever after. We win one small battle, and then we're ready to move on to the next one. We may have a few major victories that come suddenly, but not many of them. The fight to destroy Satan's strongholds comes mostly by daily, doggedly, moving ahead.

The first time I thought of that fact, it was discouraging, until I realized the wisdom of God. After the Jews left Egypt and wandered in the wilderness, God spoke to them before they went into the Promised Land. It was a special land—fertile, beautiful, and promised to them. But in the more than 400 years since Jacob and his sons had left the land, others had moved in and occupied land that didn't belong to them.

For the children of Israel, it wasn't merely a matter of going in and settling down. They had to fight for every foot of ground—even though it was their inheritance.

That's how the spiritual principle works on every level. God has the blessings out there waiting for us, but it's up to us to go in and take the land. Just as it was for the Jews of old, it is a battle.

In the verse at the beginning of this chapter, God spoke of the beasts of the field. There were many wild animals in the land, and it could have been dangerous. But what if we thought of the beasts as pride? What if God suddenly gave us full, complete victory, and we never struggled again; how would that affect us? Surely pride would creep in.

Our attitude then would be to look down on others who have not been as victorious as we have been. We may not express our condescension in words, but won't those we disdain sense that we think we're superior? And, truthfully, wouldn't we feel superior. We've made it; those poor souls are still struggling.

God has a wonderful plan for each of us, but it never comes with just one major victory, so that we never struggle again. Instead, it's an ongoing warfare, and we must remain vigilant and be aware of the attacks of the enemy.

Another aspect is that because we move ahead little by little, it makes us savor every victory. Each time we overcome or destroy one of Satan's strongholds, we rejoice. We can remain in a constant state of thanksgiving. If we've had only one victory, and that was thirty years ago, how dull our lives would be. Or worse yet, how easy it would be for us to take God for granted. Isn't it better to serve a God who takes us slowly forward, always showing us the way, always encouraging us? We always have new horizons to reach for, and that makes our journey with God exciting!

———————

God, please forgive me for wanting all the victory right now. Help me realize that as I struggle and call on You, I see Your wonderful, loving, and caring hand taking me forward—little by little. For that, I'm so grateful. Amen.

15

First the Suffering

And after you have suffered a little while, the God of all grace [Who imparts all blessing and favor], Who has called you to His [own] eternal glory in Christ Jesus, will Himself complete and make you what you ought to be, establish and ground you securely, and strengthen, and settle you.

—1 PETER 5:10

"Why do we have to suffer?" "If God truly loves us, why do all the bad things happen to us?" I hear such questions often. For thousands of years, people smarter than I am have wrestled with those questions, and they still haven't discovered the answers. I don't even try to answer the questions. I do make one comment, however: "If God **only** blessed us after we became believers—if He took away all suffering, hardship, and turmoil for Christians—wouldn't it be a way to bribe people into the faith?"

That's not the way God works. The Lord wants us to come to Him out of love and because we know we're needy—so needy that only He can fill those needs for us.

The reality is that from the time of birth until we go home

to be with Jesus, we will suffer at times. Some have harder tasks than others, but suffering is still suffering.

I also think that when people watch us as we turn to God for help in our hardships and they see our victories, it provides a witness to them. That witness may not always make them turn to Christ, but it does show God's presence in our lives and makes them aware of what they're missing.

Yes, we will suffer. The other day I had a new thought: Suffering results in thanksgiving. When our lives turn chaotic and we don't know what to do, we turn to the Lord for help, and He answers our prayers and sets us free. God speaks to us and comforts us. And the result is that we're thankful.

The time between suffering and thanksgiving is when the devil truly attacks our thoughts. He may begin by saying, "If God really loved you, you would not have to go through this." It's a subtle way of saying to us that serving God is useless. The truth is, we'll have problems if we're believers; we'll have problems if we're nonbelievers. But as believers, we'll also have victories. As believers in Jesus Christ, we can have peace in the midst of the storm. We can enjoy our lives during the hardships because we truly believe that God is working on our behalf to bring deliverance.

The next attack of Satan is to whisper, "It's not going to get better. You have served God for nothing. See, this is what happens when you really need help and trust God. He doesn't care about you. If He truly cared, why would He allow you to suffer?"

This is where we have to stand firm. We can take courage from the story of Job. Few of us have suffered as he did—he lost his children, his possessions, and his health. His critics accused him of hypocrisy and deception. Because we know how Satan works, we realize that his so-called friends were tools of Satan. I'm sure they didn't realize they were being used by the devil to discourage Job. But just because they weren't aware, doesn't mean Satan didn't use them.

However, Job, a godly man, refused to listen. He said, "[. . . though He slay me, yet will I wait for and trust Him . . .]" (Job 13:15). He refused to allow Satan to attack his mind and make him question God. He didn't understand what God had done. There's no indication that Job ever understood. But one thing he knew, God was with him and he never doubted the love and presence of God.

That's the attitude we want—that calm assurance of God's love that says, "Though He slay me, yet will I wait for and trust Him." We don't have to understand or explain. In fact, I've heard it said this way, "Obedience is required; understanding is optional."

Finally, if we suffer, it just may be a powerful reminder that we are walking the same paths as some of God's greatest saints. Even in Peter's time, they suffered. In their case, it was Roman persecution; in our case, it may be people who don't understand us, or family members who turn against us. Regardless, suffering can and should end in thanksgiving.

———————————

My Master and my God, forgive me for always wanting the easy life. I admit that I don't want to suffer, and I don't like it when things go wrong. But I ask You to help me have a good attitude and to trust You to bring good out of it. I pray this in the name of Jesus Christ. Amen.

16

No Condemnation

Therefore, [there is] now no condemnation (no adjudging guilty of wrong) for those who are in Christ Jesus, who live [and] walk not after the dictates of the flesh, but after the dictates of the Spirit.

—ROMANS 8:1

"I should have known better," Cindy cried out to me. "All the signs were there that he wasn't the man for me." She had gone through two years of a painful marriage, of verbal and finally physical abuse. Then her husband left her for another woman. Now she felt doubly condemned—condemned for marrying him in the first place and condemned that she couldn't hold the marriage together.

"If I had been a good Christian, I could have changed him," she moaned.

I could have confronted her and said, "Yes, you did see the signs and you ignored them. You opened yourself up to this kind of treatment." I didn't say those words and wouldn't. They would not have helped Cindy.

What she needed right then was for me to stretch out my hand and comfort her. She was so self-condemned that she finally asked, "Will God forgive me?"

At first, her words disturbed me. The Bible is clear that God forgives any sin. Cindy knew the Bible, so her question wasn't due to a lack of knowledge; it was due to a lack of faith in a loving, caring God. She felt so dejected, and she didn't know if God loved her enough to forgive her.

I assured Cindy of God's forgiveness, but that wasn't the real issue that troubled her. Satan had whispered in her mind for such a long time that she had failed God, that she had deliberately disobeyed, and that God was angry with her.

The devil tries to stop us every chance he gets. I often use the analogy of a baby learning to walk. We don't expect that baby to stand the first day and walk across the room like an adult. Those little ones will fall often. Sometimes they cry, but they always get back up. That may be some inborn quality, but I suspect it's because the parents are there saying, "You can do it. Come on, baby, get up and walk."

The scene is much the same in the spiritual world. All of us fall, but when we're encouraged, we get back up and try again. If we're not encouraged, we tend to stay down, or at least wait a long, long time before trying to get up again.

Never underestimate Satan's relentlessness. He will do whatever he can to trip you, and then make you feel so condemned that you won't want to get up again. He knows that his control is finished once you choose right thoughts and reject wrong ones. He wants to hinder you from clear thinking. He will attempt to thwart you through discouragement and condemnation.

I want to tell you what Cindy did. She wrote Romans 8:1 on

three 3x5 file cards and pasted one on her mirror, one on her computer, and one on her dashboard. Every time she looks at the verse, she repeats it aloud. "Therefore, [there is] now no condemnation (no adjudging guilty of wrong) for those who are in Christ Jesus, who live [and] walk not after the dictates of the flesh, but after the dictates of the Spirit."

The Message puts Romans 8:1–2 like this: "With the arrival of Jesus, the Messiah, that fateful dilemma is resolved. Those who enter into Christ's being-here-for-us no longer have to live under a continuous, low-lying black cloud. A new power is in operation. The Spirit of life in Christ, like a strong wind, has magnificently cleared the air, freeing you from a fated lifetime of brutal tyranny at the hands of sin and death."

We are free in Jesus Christ, and we don't have to listen to Satan's condemnation. When we fail—and we will—that doesn't mean we are failures. It means we failed one time in one thing. It means we didn't do everything right. That doesn't make us a failure.

"Just let Christ be strong in your weaknesses; let Him be your strength on your weak days."[1]

Lord Jesus Christ, in Your name I pray for victory. When I fail, please remind me not only that You forgive, but that You also wipe away the guilt and condemnation. Please accept my gratitude. Amen.

17

No Hope

Why are you cast down, O my inner self? And why should you moan over me and be disquieted within me? Hope in God and wait expectantly for Him, for I shall yet praise Him, my Help and my God.

—PSALM 42:5

"What's the use?" Jeff said to me. "I've tried many times to work for God and to accomplish great things. No matter what I do or how hard I work, I end up failing."

"I vowed that I would set aside time for God every day," Pam said. "That was my only resolution for the year." She shrugged. "It's now April, and I stuck with my plan for about three weeks. I never complete most of the important things in my life."

Jeff and Pam are only two examples of people who feel hopeless. They know what they want to do, but they still don't accomplish what they desire.

There is no one way we can explain all failures, but both of these believers had reached the place of hopelessness. They were sure they couldn't do it. "I've tried before, and I failed," they each said. They saw no point in trying again.

"Okay, so I try again and then I fail again," Jeff said. "I already feel bad; why would I want to feel worse?"

He didn't realize that negative thoughts and words were the cause of his own failure. Satan was there to attack and discourage him, but he did most of the work himself through an attitude of hopelessness.

"I end up failing." Those were Pam's words. "I never complete most of the important things in my life," is the way she said it.

By their own words, Jeff and Pam had prepared themselves to fail. And their words weren't the only thing that doomed them. It was the thoughts behind the words.

Discouragement destroys hope. Failure easily leads to more failure. And once we allow our minds to say, "This is the way it will always be," the devil has won a victory over us.

I urged Jeff and Pam to examine their *thought* life. "For now," I urged, "don't focus on the outcome or the result of your action. Go back to your attitude and your thought processes."

As we talked, it became obvious that Jeff expected to fail. The devil had already enslaved his mind. Of course, he failed. He got just what he expected. The same was true for Pam. Both of them thought failure and focused on failure. They expected nothing else. They were afraid they would fail right from the beginning, and the Bible says that what we fear comes upon us (see Job 3:25).

"Ask yourselves," I said, "what kind of thoughts have you been thinking?" If we change our thoughts, we can change our outcome. Jeff and Pam both believed they would fail, but I wanted them to believe they could succeed.

Jeff made great progress over the next few weeks. Whenever he started on a new project he would say, "Things are going a little slow, but I'm making progress. Yesterday was difficult, and I started to feel discouraged. I even felt a little sorry for myself. But that was because I chose wrong thinking."

The same was true for Pam. She said, "I now refuse to be discouraged. Last Tuesday night as I crawled into bed, I realized I had rushed so fast all day that I had taken no time to spend with God, and I was too tired then." She asked God to forgive her, adding, "Help me not to give up."

Pam realized that she had failed once last week and twice the week before. She reminded herself that she had been faithful the other days. That gave her hope. "It's not 100 percent victory, but it's a lot better than zero."

Both Jeff and Pam finally realized a powerful truth, and we need to understand it, too: Jesus does not condemn us; we condemn ourselves. We allow discouraging, disheartening thoughts to fill our minds. Now we need to be aware that we can push those thoughts aside and say, "With Your help, Lord Jesus, I can make it."

Lord Jesus, with Your help, I can make it. With Your help, I won't be discouraged and feel hopeless. With Your help, I can defeat every wrong thought the devil slips into my mind. Thank You for victory. Amen.

18

My Feelings

Because if you acknowledge and confess with your lips that Jesus is Lord and in your heart believe (adhere to, trust in, and rely on the truth) that God raised Him from the dead, you will be saved. For with the heart a person believes (adheres to, trusts in, and relies on Christ) and so is justified (declared righteous, acceptable to God), and with the mouth he confesses (declares openly and speaks out freely his faith) and confirms [his] salvation.

—ROMANS 10:9–10

"But I can't help the way I feel," Angie moaned.

Most of us hear this statement often. It means that the way the person feels is settled, and they believe they have to go with those feelings. It's like an unchallenged fact of life.

We have feelings, and sometimes they are strong, but we get confused. We allow our feelings to determine our decisions and, ultimately, our destiny. With that type of mindset, it means that if we *feel* discouraged, we *are* discouraged; if we *feel* victorious, we *are* victorious. It means that if we *feel* depressed, we *must be* depressed.

Someone once said, "My feelings are emotions; they are not reality." In other words, just because we feel a certain way doesn't make that feeling a fact. It only means that we feel that way. We must learn to press past our feelings.

Perhaps an example will help. Janet sells real estate, and when she makes a sale, she feels wonderful and successful. Last month she sold five upscale homes and made an excellent commission. This month she has sold only one, and she feels as if she's a failure. Is Janet a failure? No. It's just that on dark days, she *feels* that way; but that doesn't mean it's true.

Today I may not feel God at work in my life. But is that true, or is that the way I feel? I know many people who don't feel loved by God—that's how they feel, but it isn't the truth.

The devil gains a stronghold in this area. If he can convince us that our feelings are reality, he has made great progress, and we are easily defeated.

Years ago, I spoke in a church, and many people came up to me to tell me how my message had encouraged them. I beamed because I was still new in the ministry, and I really needed lots of compliments in order to feel successful. One man said, "I didn't agree with anything you said. You need to get your theology straight." And he walked away.

Immediately discouragement overwhelmed me. I had tried hard to be God's instrument to the people, and I had failed. As I left the church, I thought about what had happened. At least fifty people had told me how my words blessed them. One man came to me with a negative message. How did I react? I believed the negative. I allowed his words to shift my thinking, and I convinced myself I had failed.

I hadn't failed. I had listened to the wrong voice and allowed it to control my feelings. I determined that never again would I allow one negative voice to discourage me and make me feel that I had failed. Perhaps I had failed to help that man—and I couldn't do anything about it—but my teaching had touched many others. One woman had tears in her eyes when she told me that I had given her exactly the right word she needed to hear.

I did something else that night. I reminded myself that what I experienced had been a negative feeling, but it had not been reality. I began to quote Bible verses, reminding myself that Satan attacks us where we're weak and vulnerable. I was new to public speaking, and the man with the negative word knew that.

I thought of Romans 10:9–10. We often quote these two verses when we speak to people about their salvation; however, the principle is there no matter what the subject. Paul says that we need to believe in our heart and confess with our lips. I stopped and said aloud, "God, I believe I am in Your service. I believe I did my best for You. I believe You used my words to bless many people. I do not have to listen to that one negative voice."

Within minutes, I felt better. (See how quickly our feelings can change?) Reality hadn't changed, but I had. I refused to allow negative, wrong thinking to turn me from reality.

Loving and caring God, forgive me for thinking wrong thoughts and for allowing wrong feelings to determine my attitude. I ask You, in the name of Jesus, to help me believe Your Word and to entertain positive thoughts. Amen.

19

Positive Minds

Jesus said, Go; it shall be done for you as you have believed.
—MATTHEW 8:13

Sometimes when I stand behind the pulpit, and before I speak, I pause and my gaze sweeps across the audience. I look at the faces of the people. I love to see the bright smiles and expressions of anticipation, but there are always a few who look downtrodden and discouraged. I don't know anything about them and I don't want to judge them, but their faces look sad. They look as if they have lost hope and expect nothing positive to happen—and too often, they get exactly what they expect.

I understand those discouraged people; I was once one of them.

Here's a simple fact I've learned: Positive minds produce positive lives, but negative minds produce negative lives. The New Testament tells the story of a Roman soldier whose servant was sick, and the soldier wanted Jesus to heal him. That wasn't uncommon—many wanted Jesus to heal them or their loved ones in those days. But this soldier, instead of asking

Jesus to come to his servant, expressed his belief that if Jesus would just speak the word, his servant would be healed (see Matthew 8:8). Jesus marveled at his faith and sent out His word to heal the servant. The soldier's positive mindset—his faith—brought positive results. He expected healing, and that's exactly what happened.

Too often, we cry to Jesus to heal us, to take care of our finances, or to deliver us from problems, but we don't fully expect the good things to happen. We allow our minds to focus on the negative aspects. Doubt and unbelief war against our minds and steal our faith if we allow it.

As I wrote in my book *Battlefield of the Mind,* many years ago I was extremely negative. I used to say that if I had two positive thoughts in a row, my mind would get in a cramp. That's an exaggeration, of course, but that's how I saw myself. I lived with the same philosophy that other people have: If we don't expect anything good to happen, we won't be disappointed when it doesn't.

I could have excused my negative attitude by telling everyone about my disappointments in life—and I had many. It wasn't just my lack of expectation. It was more than that. Because I thought negatively, I spoke negatively. When people told me of their spiritual victories, I'd think, *That won't last.* When people spoke of their faith, I'd smile, but inwardly I would think that they were gullible. I could always figure out ways that plans would go wrong or people would disappoint me.

Was I happy? Of course not. Negative thinkers are never happy. It's too long of a story to explain how I came to face that reality, but once I realized what a negative person I was, I cried out to the Lord to help me.

I learned that if I kept studying the Word of God, I could push away negative thoughts. God's Word is positive and up-lifting. My responsibility was to become the kind of believer who honors God with her thoughts, as well as with her actions and her deeds.

I understood the remorse David must have felt when he wrote Psalm 51: "Have mercy upon me, O God, according to Your steadfast love . . ." is the way he starts. I especially meditated on verse 9: "Hide Your face from my sins and blot out all my guilt and iniquities." I hadn't sinned the same way David did, of course, but my negative thinking and bad attitude was sin. It wasn't just weakness or a bad habit. When I focused on negative thinking, I was rebelling against God.

The Lord had mercy on me. As I continued in His Word and in prayer, He freed me from Satan's stronghold.

Freedom is available for all of us.

Gracious God, thank You for every deliverance in my life. Thank You for setting me free from negative and wrong thinking. Thank You for defeating Satan in this area of my life. Amen.

20

A Perfect Plan

And I am convinced and sure of this very thing, that He Who began a good work in you will continue until the day of Jesus Christ [right up to the time of His return], developing [that good work] and perfecting and bringing it to full completion in you.

—Philippians 1:6

For we are God's [own] handiwork (His workmanship), recreated in Christ Jesus, [born anew] that we may do those good works which God predestined (planned beforehand) for us [taking paths which He prepared ahead of time], that we should walk in them [living the good life which He prearranged and made ready for us to live].

—Ephesians 2:10

I wonder how many times we've heard preachers say, "God has a plan for your life." We nod, perhaps smile, and then go on our way. I'm not sure most of us truly believe that—at least, our lives don't reflect that we believe it.

What does it mean to think that God has a perfect plan for us? Perhaps it's the word *perfect* that troubles us. We're fallible and make so many mistakes. How could anything be perfect in our lives? We know ourselves too well. Immediately we think of our shortcomings and shake our heads.

That's a trick of Satan! The plan isn't perfect because *we're* perfect; the plan is perfect because *God* is perfect. For now, let's say it this way: God has a *special* plan for each of our lives.

Let's think about that plan. In the previous verse, Paul told us that God saved us and started a good work in us. The Spirit is still with us, nudging us forward. Paul also wrote that we are God's handiwork (or workmanship). The two verses before that tell us that we're saved by God's grace. We have nothing to do with the act of salvation—we haven't earned it or deserved it. We are born into the kingdom of God as a gift. God does it, and we receive it. Yes, we believe, but that's not doing anything to earn our salvation.

As we think about God at work in us, we remind ourselves that, imperfect as we are, God is perfection. Nothing we can ever do would be good enough to satisfy God's perfection. Only Jesus, the Perfect One, is good enough. Nothing but our faith in Him makes us acceptable to God.

The apostle went on to say that we are saved through Jesus Christ so that we can do good works. God has prepared us for the kind of life He wants us to live. His Word makes it clear how that life works.

It's not that we're perfect or ever will be perfect while on earth. The point is that God is perfect and has a plan for us. The plan for our lives is perfect, because it comes from the Perfect Planner. God's plan for us includes obedience and service to Him from a sincere heart.

God holds out directions for a full, satisfying life. Our role is to align ourselves with that plan. We are to keep our eyes on Jesus and His ability, not on ourselves and our disabilities.

As soon as we say, "But wait! I'm not perfect! I fail," we have taken our attention off God and allowed Satan to distract us with wrong thinking. Our loving Lord pleads with us to turn our minds and hearts fully over to Him. The more fully we do that, the more completely we live by His good and perfect plan.

We are to be like Joshua, to whom God said, "This Book of the Law shall not depart out of your mouth, but you shall meditate on it day and night, that you may observe and do according to all that is written in it. For then you shall make your way prosperous, and then you shall deal wisely and have good success" (Joshua 1:8).

Perfect God, help me in this battle for my mind. Satan constantly reminds me of my imperfections and my weaknesses, but I ask You to remind me of Your perfection, Your love, and Your closeness so that I can always walk in victory. I ask these things through Jesus Christ. Amen.

21

All Things Work for Good

We are assured and know that [God being a partner in their labor] all things work together and are [fitting into a plan] for good to and for those who love God and are called according to [His] design and purpose.
—ROMANS 8:28

After John 3:16, Romans 8:28 is probably the most-quoted Bible verse among Christians. Paul's words bring comfort and peace to many of us in our difficulties and hardships. They give us hope that no matter what hurts and disappointments come in our lives, everything will eventually work out for our good.

The two verses preceding Romans 8:28 talk about prayer. They say that when we don't know how to pray as we ought to, the Holy Spirit comes to our aid and prays through us. It is through these Holy Spirit-filled prayers that all things work together for good, no matter what they are. Not all things that happen to us are good in and of themselves, but God is good and He can cause them to work toward our good if we trust Him.

Continuing to trust God is the key to victory in painful and seemingly unjust situations. Faith and prayer move the hand of God. If we continue believing, He promises to continue moving in our behalf to work everything out for good.

God makes this promise to those who love Him and are called according to His purpose. We must love God with all of our hearts, and we must want His will. We must be willing to submit to His plan at all times.

The plan that God has for us eventually changes us into His image. We are destined to be molded into His image. That may sound spiritual, but in reality, it usually hurts. I often think of clay being pressed into a mold, and wonder how the clay would feel if it had feelings. Being changed into an entirely different shape would probably be painful. If we take a lump of clay and press it into a mold, there is always too much clay to fit, and some pieces must be discarded. I found that there was more of me than would fit into the mold of Jesus Christ, so many of my thoughts, words, and actions had to be discarded.

We must go through things that are difficult and learn how to respond to them the way Jesus would. We must not give way to the fearful thoughts and feelings that attack us. We must learn to remain steadfast, knowing that no matter how things appear now, God will work them out for our good—and in the process, He will use them to make us better people.

God's purpose in everything that happens is to make us more like Jesus Christ. Jesus was the totally obedient one. "Although He was a Son, He learned [active, special] obedience through what He suffered" (Hebrews 5:8).

We also learn through what we suffer. We learn from God's Word and life's experiences. Because of our sinful nature, we tend to fight God at every point, but this only makes the process longer and more painful. Learn to surrender quickly, and save yourself a lot of agony. I've learned that God gets His way in the end, so why prolong the process?

Where the mind goes the man follows. Keep your mind going in the right direction, and your life will catch up with it. A person who has their faith firmly planted in God cannot be defeated. The Bible says that Joseph's brothers hated him, but God was with him. God gave him favor and promoted him, so we see that his faith in God lifted him above his circumstances.

Some terrible things happened to Joseph. His brothers sold him to slave traders and told his father a wild animal had killed him. He was betrayed by those whom he served and tried to help, but God was watching him all the time. God had a good plan for Joseph, and it came to pass. He ultimately said that although the things that happened to him were originally meant for harm, God intended it for good.

This same thing is true for all of us. Satan cannot defeat us if we keep believing that God is working for our good, and that we are being continually transformed into His image.

All-wise and loving God, make me more like Jesus. I don't like to suffer, and I hate to fail, but through Jesus Christ, I ask You to teach me and enable me to understand that, because of You, everything truly works together for my good. Amen.

22

Getting What We Want

Lean on, trust in, and be confident in the Lord with all your heart and mind and do not rely on your own insight or understanding. In all your ways know, recognize, and acknowledge Him, and He will direct and make straight and plain your paths.

—Proverbs 3:5–6

I usually know what I want, and I like to get it. I'm exactly like most people. When we don't get what we want, our negative feelings flare up. (And remember those feelings began with thoughts.)

"I drove across town to buy that dress, and you're out of my size?"

"What do you mean there are no HD-TVs left? You advertised it in the paper."

Most of us are like that—and when we don't get what we want, we make people around us miserable. It's not something we learn in school—it may be inborn.

As I wrote the above quotations, I thought of a scene in the grocery store. A young mother was pushing her cart along and stopped at the cereal. Her child—less than two years old—reached out for a box. "Want! Want!"

"No," the mother said. "We have plenty at home." She put a different box of cereal in the cart.

"Want! Want!" the child said. Getting no response, she began to kick and scream. To the mother's credit, she did not give in but pushed the cart to another aisle and distracted her child.

As I watched that behavior, I thought, *That's the way we all are most of the time. We decide what we want, and when we don't get it, we're angry.*

"Jack and I were both up for the same promotion. I've been with the company longer, and my sales figures are stronger," Donna said. "I deserved it, but he got the job."

"I had a grade of 98 going into my final essay test," Angie said. "If I had made another 100, it would have given me a 4.0 average, and I would have become the top student in my graduating class. But I made only 83 on the test, and dropped down to fifth in my class. I deserved a grade of 100, but my teacher doesn't like me."

Let's look at this problem more closely. The individuals mentioned above, who didn't get what they wanted, made one common statement: "I deserved it, but I didn't get it."

Too often, we Christians expect life to be perfect and for everything to go smoothly for us. We expect success, happiness, joy, peace, and everything else. When we're thwarted, we pout or complain.

Although God does want us to have a good life, there will

be times when we must be patient and endure not getting our way. These disappointments test our character and level of spiritual maturity. They actually show whether or not we truly are ready for promotion.

Why do we think we should always be first while others have to endure a lesser position? Why do we think we are entitled to the perfect life? Perhaps sometimes we think more highly of ourselves than we ought to. A humble mind enables us to take a back seat and wait for God to move us to the front. God's Word says that we inherit the promises through faith and patience. Believing God is good, but can we *continue* to believe God and trust Him when we don't feel that life is fair?

Satan plays with our minds. Most of the time, the evil one says negative things to us: "You don't deserve it; you are worthless; you're stupid." Once in a while, however, he tries a different trick: He tells us how hard we work or how much we're entitled to. If we listen and believe, we may begin to feel cheated or believe that someone has taken advantage of us.

When we don't get what we want, we fall apart, saying, "I deserved it!" We not only get angry with the boss, the teacher, or anyone else, but we sometimes get angry with God for not giving us what we felt we deserved.

The big mistake was to say we deserved it, because then self-pity creeps in when we don't get what we want. We can take that attitude, or we can recognize that we have a choice. I can choose to accept life the way it is and make the best out of it, or I can complain because it isn't perfect.

I think of the story of Jonah—not the whale story—but what happened afterward. He had announced that in forty days, God would destroy the city of Nineveh, but the people repented. Because God listened to their cries, Jonah was angry. "Therefore now, O Lord, I beseech You, take my life from me, for it is better for me to die than to live" (Jonah 4:3).

Sad, isn't it? Jonah would rather have been right than to see 120,000 people saved. Our situations aren't usually that dramatic, but so many people would rather sit and feel sorry for themselves, listen to the whispers of Satan, and miss out with God than to simply trust God in every situation.

The secret of the Christian life is that we commit ourselves fully to God. If we surrender our wills to God, what happens doesn't make us angry. If God doesn't give us what we want and ask for, our faith is strong enough to say, "Not my will, but Yours."

God, help me. I often have strong desires, and when I don't get what I want, I get upset. Forgive me. Remind me that Jesus didn't want to die on the cross, but He lived in total submission to Your will. I ask You, through Jesus Christ, to help me live in total submission and be content with what You give me. Amen.

23

No More Excuses

Therefore if any person is [ingrafted] in Christ (the Messiah) he is a new creation (a new creature altogether); the old [previous moral and spiritual condition] has passed away. Behold, the fresh and new has come!
—2 CORINTHIANS 5:17

"I've always had a bad temper. That's just the way I am."

"I'm a straightforward person. That's who I am, and that's how people need to accept me."

"I call things as I see them. I don't sugarcoat anything."

This list could go on endlessly, but the one thing these excuses have in common is that each is meant to justify the people being the way they are. It's a way of resisting change.

It's also a way for Satan to creep into our minds. The great deceiver tells us that we're not rude—we are just being honest, and people need to respect that quality in us. We think we speak the truth as we see it, and we're not cowards or hypocrites. If the devil can convince us that we don't have to change—that we're fine exactly the way we are—he has won a serious battle in our lives.

In fact, the devil can give us a lot of excuses for not changing. That may be the problem. If he convinces us that other people are at fault because "they are just too sensitive" or "they don't want to hear the truth and face reality," we don't feel responsible, and we think we're all right.

Another thing is that no matter how negative we may be in our thinking, most of us wouldn't call ourselves "negative." We prefer words like *logical, realistic, forthright,* or *candid.* Not facing the truth about ourselves is part of Satan's deceptive work.

When I went through a period of extreme negativity, I wouldn't have thought of myself as being negative. I was just being honest. If I saw something wrong, I spoke up. I offered my counsel on ways for people to change. I could see the weaknesses and problems of others, and I was quite happy to show them how they could overcome. On my worst days, I found things wrong with all my friends and everything they did. I didn't have to look for things to criticize—I did it without effort. I didn't consider it negative because I thought I was merely trying to be helpful. It never occurred to me in my prideful state that people didn't really want my help. They wanted acceptance and encouragement, not judgment and criticism.

As I said, I never thought of myself as being negative—that is, until God dealt with me and convicted me.

I'm not trying to condemn anyone for being negative, frank, blunt, candid, or whatever term you may use for it, because condemning is in itself being negative. Instead, I want to help believers recognize their attitude problems and help them realize that God is able to deliver them.

We start the Christian life as new creations of God. Our past is wiped away. The Christian life is one of change—of growth—of moving onward.

The pathway to freedom begins when we face our problems, and face them without excuses. "Yes, I'm negative, but if you had come from the kind of family, I did, you'd—"

Stop! No excuses. We know what we were in the past, but we also know that we don't have to remain that way now or in the future. With the help of Jesus Christ, we can have our minds renewed according to the Word of God.

The most difficult part may be to say to God, "I'm a negative person, but I want to change." Remember that a negative mind produces a negative life. You've probably tried to change yourself many times in the past, but it didn't work. Now you can begin to win the battle over Satan's stronghold by admitting who you are and acknowledging that you must depend on God to change you.

———————

Holy and positive God, forgive me for all my negative thinking. You want me to be loving and filled with Your joy. Help me so that Satan has no stronghold over my mind. Please destroy every negative aspect of my thinking, through Jesus my Lord. Amen.

24

Why This Negativity?

However, I am telling you nothing but the truth when I say it is profitable (good, expedient, advantageous) for you that I go away. Because if I do not go away, the Comforter (Counselor, Helper, Advocate, Intercessor, Strengthener, Standby) will not come to you [into close fellowship with you]; but if I go away, I will send Him to you [to be in close fellowship with you]. And when He comes, He will convict and convince the world and bring demonstration to it about sin and about righteousness (uprightness of heart and right standing with God) and about judgment.

—John 16:7–8

Years ago, I sat at a table with six public speakers. All of them had been in the ministry longer than I had, but God had given me more outward success than the others.

As the conversation went on, I realized I was doing most of the talking—telling one story after another. They all smiled, and no one acted as if they resented my dominating.

Afterward, I thought about my behavior. I had done nothing wrong, but I realized I had controlled the conversation, and I felt the Holy Spirit convict me. Although I wasn't aware of it at the time, in retrospect, I realized that I had been rude and selfish by dominating the conversation. Taking control— that's what I had done. Perhaps I was insecure and didn't want them to see me as anything but confident and able. I may have talked too much because I was nervous with my peers. Perhaps I was just so full of myself that all I wanted to do was talk about myself, and what I was doing. A truly loving person is interested in others and always draws them into the conversation. I realize now that I wasn't operating in love back in those days.

Most of the time, I stayed so busy talking about myself and my ministry that I never faced what was wrong inside me. I felt a little nudge from the Holy Spirit frequently, but I never really stopped to pay much attention.

Instead of looking at our own shortcomings and failures, we often focus on other people and what we think is wrong with them. That's easier and less painful. As long as we can keep the focus on other people, we don't have to examine our own hearts.

It's not calculated, and I'm sure most of us are not aware of the reasons for our being negative. That's also why negativity is so difficult to deal with. We undermine Satan's attempt to establish a stronghold in our minds when we admit, "God, I'm a pessimistic person." That's the beginning.

Then we cry out to the Holy Spirit to search our hearts. Jesus said of Him, ". . . He will convict and convince the world and bring demonstration to it about sin and about righteousness (uprightness of heart and right standing with

God) and about judgment" (John 16:8). Too often, we read the word *world* and smile. Yes, that's for those sinners, those people who don't know Jesus. That's true, but it's only partially true, because we also live in the world.

We—God's people—need that conviction, as well. We need the Holy Spirit to probe deeply inside us and help us grasp why we're afflicted with negative thinking. We probably know many nonbelievers who are naturally optimistic, and who never speak badly about others. Satan already has control of their minds, so he doesn't even tempt them to be negative.

Think of it this way: Satan attacks us where we're weak. Perhaps this will help explain what I mean. More than 100 years ago, William Sheldon began to study human body types and classified them as distinct types. His research indicated that all of us are prone toward certain types of physical diseases. Those with the pear-shaped figure are more prone to heart problems and high blood pressure. I have a rail-thin friend, and when she gets sick, she comes down with a lung infection or bronchitis. She's in her seventies, has a healthy heart, and is otherwise healthy—but she has weak lungs.

Let's apply that principle to the spiritual realm. All of us have weaknesses—some of us are prone to pessimism, some to lying or gossip, others are by nature more deceptive. It's not which person is worse, because all of us have our own weaknesses to conquer. We need the Holy Spirit to point out these shortcomings. Just because those are the natural places for Satan's attacks doesn't mean we can do nothing about them. Only as the Spirit convicts us can He deliver us from satanic attacks. That's why Jesus sent the Holy Spirit—the Helper—because He helps us in our vulnerable places.

Holy Spirit of God, forgive me for thinking I can deliver myself. Don't allow Satan to take advantage of my vulnerability, but deliver me so that I may be more fully given to You and used by You. I ask this through the name of my Savior, Jesus. Amen.

25

Ready Minds

Now these [Jews] were better disposed and more noble than those in Thessalonica, for they were entirely ready and accepted and welcomed the message [concerning the attainment through Christ of eternal salvation in the kingdom of God] with inclination of mind and eagerness, searching and examining the Scriptures daily to see if these things were so.

—ACTS 17:11

One of my much-published writer friends taught a series of classes at a writers' conference on beginning writing. He wanted to reach people who felt God had called them to write and show them how to get their articles and books published.

At the beginning, he asked the attendees how long they had been writing and if they had ever published. Two women, who sat in the front row, said they had both been writing for almost twelve years, but had not yet published anything.

At the end of the first lecture, my friend overheard one of

the women say to the other, "Oh, we know all of that. We don't need to come back to this class."

They may have already known the things he was teaching, but there was no evidence they had applied what they knew. He also commented that the most eager students in the classroom were those who had already begun to publish. They wanted to learn and improve. Only people who are humble enough to continue learning will ever succeed.

That incident makes me think of an event in the book of Acts. The apostles Paul and Silas preached in Thessalonica, and the people tried to kill them, so believers helped them flee. From there, they went to the city of Berea. Luke records that the people there were fair in their thinking. They received the message "with all readiness," or, as I like to say, they had ready minds.

That means those were people who were open to God— they were willing to hear what God said, no matter whether it was good news or bad.

If I asked any group of Christians, "Are you ready-minded?" they would immediately say that they were. That's what we assume being a Christian means—ready, open, willing to hear God, and to be obedient to what He says.

For many people, being ready-minded means that they are ready and open if the message is what they want to hear. If it's not what they want to hear, they don't try to kill the messengers like the Thessalonians, but they say, "Oh, we know all of that," and stop listening.

What does it really mean to be ready-minded? It means being willing to turn away from every lie and deception that Satan offers. It means being willing to say, "I was wrong." It means that instead of listening only for what we want to hear, we listen for what we need to hear.

To be ready-minded means we discern the source of the voice. We love to hear words that make us feel good and encourage us, but we don't like words that make us aware of our shortcomings. In Satan's battle for our minds, one of his tricks is to convince us that a message isn't important or that we already know it. He may even say that the message is not correct, and by doing so, he prevents us from hearing what we really need in order to gain our own freedom.

For example, a pastor preached a sermon against gossip one day. He aimed his message at one woman—who delighted in telling people tales about others. What she didn't know, she allowed her imagination to fill in. At the end of the service, she said to the pastor, "That was an excellent message. A lot of people in this church need to hear that."

The pastor said she wasn't being sarcastic or hypocritical. She simply didn't get the message. She didn't have that ready mind—the mind that was open to receive a message of grace and help from God. It never occurred to her that *she* needed the message. To have a ready mind is not always easy. In fact, the more seriously the Holy Spirit wants to deal with us, the more Satan tries to convince us that we already "know all that" or it's not something we need to hear.

Lord Jesus, please give me a ready mind. Enable me to hear You clearly and easily. Enable me to say, "Yes, Lord," no matter what Your Spirit has to say to me. I want to have a ready mind that pleases You in everything. I ask this in Your name. Amen.

26

Positive Belief

*[For Abraham, human reason for] hope being gone, hoped in
faith that he should become the father of many nations, as he
had been promised, so [numberless] shall your descendants
be. He did not weaken in faith when he considered the [utter]
impotence of his own body, which was as good as dead
because he was about a hundred years old, or [when he
considered] the barrenness of Sarah's [deadened] womb. No
unbelief or distrust made him waver (doubtingly question)
concerning the promise of God, but he grew strong and was
empowered by faith as he gave praise and glory to God, fully
satisfied and assured that God was able and mighty to keep
His word and to do what He had promised.*
—Romans 4:18–21

The story of Abraham amazes me no matter how many times
I read it. It's not just the birth of a son when he was a hundred
years old. That's a miracle. But just as amazing is the information that he waited twenty-five years for the fulfillment of the
promise. He was seventy-five when God promised him a son.

I wonder how many of us would believe God and live in
expectation for twenty-five years. Most of us probably would
have said, "I didn't really hear from God." "Oh, I guess maybe

God didn't really mean that." Or, "I need to go somewhere else to get a fresh word from the Lord."

Sarah and Abraham did have problems holding on to that promise. As a means of attempting to get what they wanted, they had Sarah's handmaiden, Hagar, bear him a son, but God let him know that wasn't the way it was going to be. I believe their actions delayed the arrival of God's promised child.

In our impatience, we often take matters into our own hands. I say we get "bright ideas"—plans of our own, which we hope God will bless. These plans open the door for confusion and chaos. Then their results must be dealt with, which often delays our miracle.

When Moses came down from Sinai after having received the Ten Commandments from God, He saw the wickedness of the Israelites who had become impatient in waiting. In anger, he broke the tablets on which God had written the commands. Although we can understand Moses' anger, we must remember that it was not initiated by God. Therefore, Moses had to ascend Mount Sinai again and once more go through the process of obtaining the Ten Commandments. Moses may have enjoyed a momentary emotional release, but it cost him a lot of extra work. This is a good lesson for all of us. We must pray first and agree with God's plan, not plan and pray that our plan will work.

It's often difficult to believe God and hold on year after year after year.

Sometimes after my meetings, people come to me and tell me many sad stories. I encourage them to become positive and upbeat. Some people will listen to every word I say, nod, maybe even smile, and then they say the most negative word of all: "But . . ." With that single word, they are negating everything I've said. That's not the spirit of Abraham.

The Bible gives us promises, hope, and encouragement. God promises good to those of us who serve Him. Despite the adversity of our circumstances—and some people have absolutely terrible situations—God still promises good. Our sense of goodness, however, may not be the same as God's. Getting what we want immediately may not be best for us. Sometimes waiting is the best thing because it helps develop the character of God in us.

The Lord chooses to do good to us and to make us happy; the devil chooses to do wrong and to make us miserable. We can remain patient and keep believing God's promises, or we can allow the evil one's whisper to fill our ears and lead us astray.

Too many of us have ignored the fact that God is the originator of miracles. He specializes in doing the impossible: He provided a son to barren Sarah; He opened the Red Sea for the Israelites to walk across on dry land; He destroyed Goliath with a single stone from a slingshot. Those are miracles. That's the Holy Spirit at work, defying the laws of nature (He made the laws, so He can break them).

Hebrews 11 is a chapter about faith and the people of God who dared to believe the promises. "But without faith it is impossible to please and be satisfactory to Him. For whoever would come near to God must [necessarily] believe that God exists and that He is the rewarder of those who earnestly and diligently seek Him [out]" (v. 6).

As I consider that verse, I can see how the devil creeps in. He says to us, "Yes, that's true. Those were *special* people. You are nobody. God won't do anything special for you. Why should He?"

That is a satanic lie—and one that too many easily accept. God loves each of us, and the Bible says He's our Father. Any good father loves to do good things for his children. God wants to do good things for you and for me.

Expect a miracle in your life. Expect many miracles.

Positive belief in God's promises yields good results because the Good One sends them to us. Refuse to give up, and you will see the result of your positive belief.

———————

Dear Father in heaven, forgive my lack of belief. Forgive me for allowing Satan to deceive me or make me think I'm worthless or unworthy of Your miracles. I am worthy because You made me worthy. You are the God of the impossible, and I ask You to help me wait on You and never give up. In the name of Jesus Christ my Lord, I pray. Amen.

27

The Waiting God

And therefore the Lord [earnestly] waits [expecting, looking, and longing] to be gracious to you; and therefore He lifts Himself up, that He may have mercy on you and show loving-kindness to you. For the Lord is a God of justice. Blessed (happy, fortunate, to be envied) are all those who [earnestly] wait for Him, who expect and look and long for Him [for his victory].

—ISAIAH 30:18

This verse has become one of my favorites, and it has often been a source of encouragement to me when I've had hard times. *The Living Bible* paraphrases the verse like this: "Yet the Lord still waits for you to come to him, so he can show you his love; he will conquer you to bless you, just as he said. For the Lord is faithful to his promises. Blessed are all those who wait for him to help them." Let's think of the implication of the promise. God waits for *us*. As I think of that promise, it staggers my mind. The Creator of the universe and the Giver of all life has chosen to wait for us—waits for us to come to our senses, waits for us to respond to His love, waits for us to turn to Him for help.

That's a staggering thought. God wants to show us love.

Perhaps as much as anywhere else, Satan attempts to build a mental stronghold right there. When we contemplate God's love for us, many of us can't take it in. We can only think of our failures, our shortcomings, and dozens of other reasons why God shouldn't love us.

That reminds me of a kind man I've known for many years. One day he took care of a situation for me that he didn't have to. I was surprised and deeply touched. "You are probably the kindest man I know," I told him.

He stared at me in shock. "Me? Kind? Oh, I can be mean-spirited and cruel," he said. For several minutes, he explained to me that he couldn't possibly be a kind man. "I live with myself all the time, and I see all my defects."

"Maybe that's the trouble," I told him. "You see your defects so clearly, you don't see your caring, compassionate qualities. You discount all those things."

He never could accept that he was kind. I also used the word *gentle* and that surprised him, too.

Perhaps that's how it is with many of God's people. We are so absorbed by our failures and all the wrong things we see about ourselves, it's hard to believe that God wants to bless us. If we read, "God wants to punish you," we wouldn't have trouble saying, "Yes, that's what I deserve."

But how would we answer if someone said, "God wants to bless you"? We probably would say, "I don't deserve that."

How many of us believe we are entitled to God's blessings? We want the good things. We want God to love us, encourage us, bless us, and give us victory, but to say we *deserve* the blessings may be more than we are willing to accept.

Why do we struggle over the concept of deserving? Our tendency is to think that we have to do something to earn the blessings . . . that we have to be good enough or faithful enough. We miss the point of God's powerful, gracious love. Our blessings from God are not a result of *our* goodness. They are the result of *God's* goodness.

We are entitled to God's blessings for only one reason: because we are His children. It's just that simple. Those of us who are parents grasp that concept with regard to our children. We brought them into the world, and they deserve our love. We freely give them our love before they do anything good or bad. They deserve our protection and all the good things we choose to give them. They don't deserve those things because they've done something to earn them, but simply because they are our children.

Satan loves to trip us up on this one. As soon as we think it is right for us to be blessed, he points to our weaknesses or our failures. God points to our relationship. That's the difference.

———————

Gracious and loving God, thank You for being willing to bless me. Even though the devil tries to make me feel undeserving, please remind me that I am Your child and You are my Father. My relationship to You makes me deserving, and I thank You for that in the name of Jesus Christ. Amen.

28

Evil Forebodings

All the days of the desponding and afflicted are made evil [by anxious thoughts and forebodings], but he who has a glad heart has a continual feast [regardless of circumstances].
—Proverbs 15:15

Shortly after I began to seriously study the Bible, I felt an oppressive atmosphere around me. Everything seemed gloomy—as if something bad was going to happen. It wasn't anything I could explain, just a vague, dreaded sense of something evil or wrong about to happen.

"Oh, God," I prayed. "What's going on? What is this feeling?"

I had hardly uttered the question when God spoke to me. "Evil forebodings."

I had to meditate on that for several minutes. I had never heard the phrase before. God had spoken to me, and I stayed quiet before Him so I could hear the answers.

I realized, first of all, that my anxieties weren't real—that is, they were not based on true circumstances or situations. I was having problems—as most of us do —but they were not as critical as the devil was making it appear. My acceptance of his lies, even though they were vague, was opening the door for the evil forebodings. I eventually realized that I had lived in the midst of similar gloomy feelings most of my life. I was expecting something bad to happen instead of aggressively expecting something good.

I felt a dread, an unexplained anxiety around me. I couldn't put my finger on anything specific—only that sense of something evil or terrible.

The Living Bible says, "When a man is gloomy, everything seems to go wrong." That's how I felt, as if something—maybe everything—was wrong or was about to go wrong.

As previously stated, I realized that for most of my life, I had been miserable because of evil thoughts and anxious forebodings.

As I continued to meditate on evil forebodings, God broke through and gave me a clear revelation. *I was miserable because my thoughts were miserable*—my thoughts were poisoning my outlook. My thoughts robbed me of the ability to enjoy my life. I should have been saying, "Thank You, God, for today. Thank you for Dave and my children and my friends and all Your blessings." But, instead of being positive, I found myself even dreading to answer the phone when it rang, for fear it might be bad news.

All of this gloom and doom that surrounded me began in my abusive childhood. I endured a great deal of misery, and most of my life was unhappy and filled with disappointments. I began to live in a vague fear and dread of the future.

I had not been taught to let go of what was behind. I couldn't rejoice in what I had now and the good things going on in my life. I focused on the past and what might lie ahead—and what lay ahead was usually gloom and doom and chaos because that was what I was expecting. Satan had built a stronghold in my mind, and I was trapped until I learned I could tear down that negative, evil stronghold by applying God's Word to my life and circumstances.

I once had a friend whom I'll call Marlene. She lived in a state of constant chaos. One day she had health problems. The next day Marlene's son had lost his job, and they were going to have to support him and his family. As soon as that was over, another traumatic situation would erupt. Marlene was a Christian, but she lived in fear of bad news. Marlene would not have known how to live a life that was not filled with chaos. All of her conversation was negative and gloomy. Even her countenance was sad and gloomy.

I realized that I had started to become like Marlene—I was miserable because I had allowed Satan to rob me of the ability to enjoy my life. It took a while before I was able to be positive most of the time, but little by little, my thinking changed, and so did my life. I no longer live in evil forebodings, expecting to hear at any moment of a new problem. Now I purposely expect good things to happen in my life. I realize now that I can choose my thoughts. I don't have to accept Satan's lies.

Like everyone else, negative things do happen to me from

time to time, but I don't become negative because of them. I remain positive, and that helps me enjoy my life even in the midst of the storms.

———————————

Dear Lord Jesus, through so many days in my life, I have been robbed of my joy and contentment by evil forebodings. As those feelings come to me, please remind me that You are in control. Help me to rest in You and rejoice in Your power in my life. Amen.

29

Hold Your Tongue

*Keep your tongue from evil and your lips from speaking
deceit. Depart from evil and do good; seek, inquire for, and
crave peace and pursue (go after) it!*
—Psalm 34:13–14

"You really have the gift of gab," one man told me many
years ago, when I first started in the ministry. He had pointed
out something that I already knew: God had given me "a
ready tongue," that is, I speak easily. Words are my tools. The
Lord first gave me that gift, and then He called me into the
ministry to use that ability to work for Him.

I have no trouble talking. That's my gift; that's also been
my greatest problem. Because I seem to always have something to say, I have struggled many, many years over the right
use of my tongue.

It has not been an easy battle.

Over the years, I heard various people saying things like,
"Hold your tongue." "Do you have to speak every word that
comes to your mind?" "Do you always speak first and think
later?" "Must you sound so harsh?" Had I truly listened to

what people were saying, I might have realized that God was trying to tell me something. But I ignored their comments and continued in my own stubborn ways.

I know I have wounded people with my words in the past, and I am sorry for that. I'm also grateful that God has forgiven me.

Several years ago, I realized that if God was going to use my life, I had to gain control of my tongue—not to just stop talking, but to keep my tongue from evil, and my lips from speaking deceit, as the psalmist David says.

I had a choice. I could hurt people with my words—and I could do that well—or I could bring my lips into subjection to God. Obviously, I wanted to be subject to the Lord, but it was still a battle.

Our words are expressions of our hearts—of what's going on inside us. If we want to know who a person really is, all we need to do is listen to their words. If we listen long enough, we learn a lot about them.

As I learned to listen to my own words, I also began to learn a lot about myself. Some of the things I learned did not please me, but they did help me realize that I had a character flaw that needed to be addressed. My words were not pleasing God, and I wanted them to. Once I confessed my failure to God, the victory came—not all at once and not perfectly, but God is patient with me. I'm growing, and part of my growth is keeping my lips from evil.

No matter how negative you are or have been, or how long you've been that way, God wants to change you. In the early days after my confession to God, I still failed more often than I succeeded, but every time I did succeed, I knew I was closer to God's plan for my life. God can do the same for you.

It won't be easy, but you can win. And the effort will be worth it.

———————————

Lord, help me use my mouth for right things. Put a watch over my mouth lest I sin against You with my tongue. Let the words of my mouth and the meditation of my heart be acceptable to You. I ask it in Jesus' wonderful name. Amen.

30

Mind-Binding Spirits

He sends forth His word and heals them and rescues them from the pit and destruction.

—Psalm 107:20

I knew God had called me to a powerful, worldwide ministry. I didn't brag about it and didn't feel that I was special. I knew I was just a woman from Fenton, Missouri, whom no one had ever heard of. Yet I believed I would have a national radio ministry. I believed God would use me to heal the sick and to change lives.

In fact, instead of being proud, I was humbled. Who was I that God would use me? The more I meditated on that idea, the more I rejoiced in the goodness and sovereignty of God. In 1 Corinthians 1:26-31, the apostle Paul pointed out that God's choices often appear mysterious. He chooses the foolish to dumbfound the wise, the weak to shame the mighty. Paul concluded, "Let him who boasts and proudly rejoices and glories, boast and proudly rejoice and glory in the Lord" (v. 31).

I felt no cause to boast. I believed God's calling and

promise to me. That's what I want to stress. And then I waited for God to open the doors that no one could shut. When He was ready, it would happen.

Although I don't know when the problem began, one day I heard myself ask, "I wonder if God really does want to use me?" Instead of holding on to the promises of God, I looked at myself and my lack of qualifications. I started to compare myself with other servants of God. When you compare yourself with others, that's always a mistake, because you usually end up on the negative side.

Doubts began to creep in. *Maybe I just made that up. Maybe I wanted something like that to happen, but it probably won't.* The longer the predicament went on, the more confused I became. I questioned God and the promise. I realized I no longer had the bright vision God had given me. I was filled with doubt and unbelief.

I began to pray and plead with God to help me. "If I just made up the things I have believed that You called me to do, then take the desire away. But if You've truly called me, help me. Restore the vision."

When I paused, I heard God speak in my heart, *Mindbinding spirits.*

"What's a mind-binding spirit?" I asked. I had never heard the term, so I didn't think anything more about it.

The next day when I prayed, I heard the same words. In fact, every time I prayed for the next two days, I heard, *Mindbinding spirits.*

I had already done a lot of ministry, and I had long realized how much trouble many believers had with their minds. At first, I thought the Holy Spirit might be leading me to pray for the Body of Jesus Christ to stand against a spirit called Mind Binding.

I prayed and I rebuked that spirit—and then I realized those words were for me. A mind-binding spirit had tried to steal my vision, destroy my joy, and take away my ministry. A tremendous deliverance came over me.

The oppressiveness was gone; the questions had vanished. I was free, and the vision of the national ministry God had given me was central in my thoughts again. I read Psalm 107:20: "He sends forth His word and heals them and rescues them from the pit and destruction." That was it!

An evil spirit was attacking my mind and preventing me from believing the promise of God. I asked God to help me, and He set me free.

That mind-binding spirit attacks many today. They know what God wants and are eager to serve. Sometimes they even announce God's plans to their friends. When nothing happens immediately, the mind-binding spirit sneaks in. It is as if a band of iron snaps around their minds and they find it hard to believe that their dreams can come to pass. Satan whispers, "Did God really say that? Or did you just make it up?" Hold fast. If God has spoken, God will perform it. Remember that Abraham waited twenty-five years for God to give him Isaac!

True and faithful God, forgive me when I allow doubts and confusion to creep into my thinking. Those are not Your tools. Through the powerful name of Jesus, enable me to break the power of every mind-binding spirit. Amen.

31

Decide to Believe

Consider it wholly joyful, my brethren, whenever you are enveloped in or encounter trials of any sort or fall into various temptations. Be assured and understand that the trial and proving of your faith bring out endurance and steadfastness and patience. But let endurance and steadfastness and patience have full play and do a thorough work, so that you may be [people] perfectly and fully developed [with no defects], lacking in nothing.

—James 1:2–4

Too often people stare at me with a blank look when I urge them to decide to believe. It's as if I'm asking them to do something they can't do. Faith comes from hearing the Word of God (see Romans 10:17), but it also involves a decision.

We enter into a relationship with God through believing in Jesus Christ, but that's only the beginning.

Believing doesn't end there. As I understand the realm of the Spirit, if we follow the Lord, we live with a growing faith. That means we learn to believe for bigger things. We learn to trust God for things we would never have thought of in our earliest Christian days.

When we become Christians, the Bible says we are adopted into the family of God: ". . . but you have received the Spirit of adoption [the Spirit producing sonship] in . . . which we cry, Abba (Father)! Father!" (Romans 8:15b).

That's the beginning. That's also where too many Christians stop. The Spirit keeps reaching for your hands so He can pull you forward. That's when you must decide to believe—or you resist and stay exactly where you are in your Christian experience.

Read the verse at the beginning of this topic. It says your faith will be tested, but you must hold onto it and move forward. The testing may come when the devil attempts to make you doubt the promises God has given you.

There is never a stopping place in your spiritual growth—God wants to take you onward. But you have to make the choice to believe. Sometimes that takes courage, but that's how the Christian life functions. We grow by taking steps of faith.

When God speaks to your heart—to your inner being—you need to learn to say without hesitation, "Let it be so, Lord." You have to learn to agree with whatever the Spirit of God says or wants.

Instead, many tend to resist. They don't say no. Satan is too subtle to nudge them to do that. He puts questions in their minds, urging them to ask, "How can that be?" They start asking God to help them *understand.* If your boss wants you to do a task, you can ask, "Why?"or ask for an explanation.

But that is not how the Holy Spirit works. You say, "Lord, if

You'll help me understand, I will believe and obey." God says, "Just obey. If I want you to understand, I'll make it clear to you." God doesn't have to explain anything to us.

It frequently happens that believers *know* something down deep in their hearts—in their inner beings—but their minds fight against it. They may consider themselves unworthy. They may ask, "Who am I that You would use me to change lives?" They waste a lot of energy by telling God why they can't do what He wants them to do. God already knows everything that is wrong with us or ever will be wrong with us, and He is willing to work through us anyway. God requires availability not ability.

God asks you to do something quite simple: Believe. That's all. If God speaks, you need to learn to say, "Even though I don't understand, I'll do it." One of the best examples I can think of in Scripture is the story of Ananias of Damascus. God told him that Saul (later called Paul) was blind and in a particular house. He was to go and lay hands on him, and God would heal him (see Acts 9:10–19).

Ananias was afraid. Saul was the great persecutor of Christians, but God told him to go because the blinded man was a chosen vessel. Despite his fear and inability to understand why God would choose a great persecutor to be a chosen vessel, Ananias went and prayed for Saul, and the future apostle was healed.

That's how God wants us to behave. He wants us to choose to believe Him even if what He's asking us to do doesn't compute in our thoughts.

Holy Spirit of God, help me always to believe Your promises, even when I don't understand Your purpose. I want to learn to trust You more, as I move forward in faith to accomplish what You have for me to do. Help me always to be obedient, in Jesus' name I pray. Amen.

32

Be Careful What You Think

But his delight and desire are in the law of the Lord, and on His law (the precepts, the instructions, the teachings of God) he habitually meditates (ponders and studies) by day and by night. And he shall be like a tree firmly planted [and tended] by the streams of water, ready to bring forth its fruit in its season; its leaf also shall not fade or wither; and everything he does shall prosper [and come to maturity].

—PSALM 1:2–3

Your word have I laid up in my heart, that I might not sin against You . . . I will meditate on Your precepts and have respect to Your ways [the paths of life marked out by Your law].

—PSALM 119:11, 15

In the early days of computers, they used to say, "Garbage in, garbage out." That was a way of explaining that the computer only worked with the data put into the machine. If we wanted different results, we needed to put in different information.

With computers, most people have no trouble grasping that concept, but when it comes to their minds, they don't seem to get it. Or perhaps they don't *want* to get it. So many things demand their attention and beg for their focus. They're not just sinful things. The apostle Paul said that although everything was lawful for him, not everything was helpful (see 1 Corinthians 6:12).

If you are going to win the battle of the mind and defeat your enemy, where you focus your attention is crucial. The more you meditate on God's Word, the stronger you'll become and the more easily you'll win the victories.

Too many Christians don't realize the difference between meditating on the Bible and reading the Bible. They like to think that whenever they read God's Word, they're absorbing the deep things of God. Too often people will read a chapter of the Bible, and when they get to the last verse, they have little idea of what they've read. Those who meditate on God's Word are those who think—and think seriously—about what they're reading.

They may not put it in these words, but they are saying, "God, speak to me. Teach me. As I ponder Your Word, reveal its depth to me."

On the previous page, I quoted from Psalm 1. This psalm begins by defining the person who is blessed, and then points out the right actions of that person. The psalmist wrote that those who meditate—and do it day and night—are like productive trees . . . and everything they do shall prosper.

The psalmist made it quite clear that meditating on and thinking about God's Word brings results. As you ponder who God is and what He's saying to you, you'll grow. It's really that simple. Another way to put it is to say that whatever you focus on, you become. If you read about and allow your mind to focus on God's love and power, that's what operates in you.

The apostle Paul says it beautifully in Philippians 4:8: ". . . Whatever is true, whatever is worthy of reverence and is honorable and seemly, whatever is just, whatever is pure, whatever is lovely and lovable, whatever is kind and winsome and gracious, if there is any virtue and excellence, if there is anything worthy of praise, think on and weigh and take account of these things [fix your minds on them]."

It's sad, but most Christians don't put much effort into their study of the Word. They go to hear others teach and preach, and they may listen to sermon tapes and read the Bible occasionally, but they're not dedicated to making God's Word a major part of their lives.

Be careful what you think about. The more you think about good things, the better your life will seem. The more you think about Jesus Christ and the principles He taught, the more you become like Jesus and the stronger you grow. And as you grow, you win the battle for your mind.

———————————

Lord God, help me think about the things that honor You. Fill my life with a hunger for more of You and Your Word so that in everything I may prosper. I ask this through Jesus Christ. Amen.

33

Meditation Produces Success

My son, give attention to my words; Incline your ear to my sayings. Do not let them depart from your eyes; Keep them in the midst of your heart; For they are life to those who find them, and health to all their flesh.

—PROVERBS 4:20–22 NKJV

When we refer to "meditating," we mean we ponder something and give it our full attention. A French couple helped me see that meditation is like eating. They will take a bite of food after they have enjoyed the way it looks on the plate. They comment on the pleasant aroma and often mention one or two special ingredients. They chew slowly and deliberately, and they sometimes even comment on how it makes the inside of their mouth feel.

That seems a bit too much for most Americans, but that's a good picture of meditating on God's Word. We don't just wolf down a few words or a verse and hurry on to the next. We pause to reflect on a word, a phrase, or a concept. We compare that scripture with others that come to mind. We feel in no hurry to dash to the end of the chapter. The words are there for us to savor and enjoy. We should learn to be more concerned about quality than quantity. It is more important to get a deep understanding of one verse of Scripture than it is to read five chapters and understand nothing.

Meditating on God's Word demands discipline. We live in such a fast-paced world that few of us make time to meditate. We should form a habit of setting aside time just to sit and think about God's Word and the wonderful promises He has made to those who believe in Him. The blessed person mentioned in Psalm 1 is the person who meditates on God's Word "by day and by night." The expression "by day and by night" means that it is a major part of a person's life. It's a way of saying that thinking about the Word of God should be a regular part of daily activity. This will require casting down wrong thoughts when they come and choosing to think on things that will benefit us. If we keep ourselves focused, it pays off spiritually.

I spend time with God in prayer and in study of His Word each morning, but I also apply the Word to situations that I deal with all throughout the day. During the writing of this devotion, I got some bad news by phone, and my response was to quote and think about various promises in God's Word. His Word strengthens us and helps us keep our peace and joy.

I titled this "Meditation Produces Success" because it's important for us to understand that contemplating the meaning of Scripture isn't simply a good thing to do or an activity reserved for scholars. It's God's command to all of us. It is a requirement for true success.

I thought of the instructions to Joshua as he prepared to lead the people into the Promised Land. The first few verses of the book of Joshua provide God's direction for him. There were at least two million people going into the land, and the responsibility of leading them was immense.

God promised to be with Joshua as He was with Moses, and He urged the new leader to be very courageous. Then He said, "This Book of the Law shall not depart out of your mouth, but you shall meditate on it day and night, that you may observe and do according to all that is written in it. For then you shall make your way prosperous, and then you shall deal wisely and have good success" (Joshua 1:8).

The instructions seem clear. Joshua had the commands of God, and his primary responsibility was to contemplate those words. By immersing himself in the law, he was learning to understand the mind of God more fully. God went on to say that if Joshua kept his mind and heart on the law, he would be prosperous and successful.

Too often people focus on their problems instead of meditating on God's promises. As they do, their problems seem to get bigger, and God's power diminishes.

God doesn't want Satan to fill your mind. He doesn't want you to give him the opportunity to inject wrong and negative thoughts into your head. For the devil to control your life, all he needs to do is to control your thoughts. Make a decision right now that you will not allow him to do that. Don't let him defeat you.

Father God, You have told me to meditate on Your Word, and I ask You to help me do that. I want Your Word to be the focus of my life. When problems come, help me turn to Your Word immediately. When Satan attacks my mind, remind me to counterattack with Your Word. As I meditate on Your Word regularly, I believe I will see good progress in my life. I ask this in Jesus' name. Amen.

34

"I Want a Mind Change"

And you [He made alive], when you were dead (slain) by [your] trespasses and sins in which at one time you walked [habitually]. You were following the course and fashion of this world [were under the sway of the tendency of this present age], following the prince of the power of the air. [You were obedient to and under the control of] the [demon] spirit that still constantly works in the sons of disobedience [the careless, the rebellious, and the unbelieving, who go against the purposes of God].

—Ephesians 2:1–2

I find a great deal of comfort in thinking about who I used to be and who I have become. It helps me not to be discouraged when I make mistakes or find that I still struggle over some issues. I'm greatly encouraged when I consider where I started and where I am now.

In Ephesians 2, Paul described those outside of Christ. He wrote that unbelievers follow the prince of the power of the air, who is Satan, and they follow the way their master leads. In verse 1, he pointed out that all were once dead through their sins, but believers are now alive in Jesus Christ. He tells us we're not governed or led by our lower nature—the impulses of the flesh.

Many Christians have trouble in this area because they haven't learned to control their thoughts. A lady once told me, "It simply didn't occur to me that I needed to direct my mind and keep it healthy and positive. If ministers preached or taught about the control of our thoughts, I never heard it. One day, however, I read an article about the power of thoughts, and God convicted me. That's when I knew I needed to change my thinking."

This lady said she drove down the street of a busy city and she spotted a sign, a cartoon of a car with big eyes for the front lights and tears flowing, and the words, "Please help me! I need an oil change."

As she passed by, she thought, *I need a mind change. I don't like being the way I am, letting my mind go wherever it wants. Part of my responsibility as a child of God is to keep my thoughts healthy and strong.*

"I want to make it clear that I went to church," she said, "and I had been active for years. I knew a lot of Scripture, and I even did some volunteer work at the church. But I didn't control my thoughts. Even when I sang in church, my mind jumped from subject to subject. We'd be singing about joy and grace, and I'd think about the dishes still in the sink, the unfinished laundry, or what I wanted to eat for lunch.

"I attended church and I was faithful, but I was not faithful in attending to the Word. I listened when the preachers quoted Scripture. I usually followed along with my own

Bible, but I didn't really think about what I was hearing or what my eyes were reading. I was doing the right things outwardly, but I wasn't thinking the right things. My mind was a mess, and I didn't know what to do about it."

"I need a mind change," she suddenly said aloud to herself. Just then, she actually pondered the words she had spoken. She was like the car on the sign—she needed a change—a mind change. She needed to let the Holy Spirit direct her thoughts instead of the devil. As she prayed, she felt confident there would be a positive change.

She thought to herself, *Is there anything I am supposed to do?* She realized that if she didn't make lifestyle changes, the devil would soon make the new thinking as muddy and gunky as the old thinking was.

For the next several days, she looked up all the scriptures she could find that used the word *study* or *meditate*. She also looked up scriptures that talked about the mind or thoughts. She read those verses, wrote them on slips of paper, and pondered them.

Here are three of them.

"For as he thinks in his heart, so is he . . ." (Proverbs 23:7 NKJV).

"And be constantly renewed in the spirit of your mind [having a fresh mental and spiritual attitude]" (Ephesians 4:23).

"My hands also will I lift up [in fervent supplication] to Your commandments, which I love, and I will meditate on Your statutes" (Psalm 119:48).

The more she meditated on the right things, the less trouble she had with Satan trying to control her thoughts. That's how it works with all of us: The more we focus on God, the less often the devil can defeat us.

———————

Thank You, great God, for giving me a mind change. Help me always to be free to serve You with my heart, my soul, and my *mind.* In the mighty name of Jesus Christ, I pray. Amen.

35

A Transformed Mind

*Do not be conformed to this world (this age), [fashioned after
and adapted to its external, superficial customs], but be
transformed (changed) by the [entire] renewal of your mind
[by its new ideals and its new attitude], so that you may
prove [for yourselves] what is the good and acceptable and
perfect will of God, even the thing which is good and
acceptable and perfect [in His sight for you].*
—ROMANS 12:2

Paul used two interesting words in Romans 12:2. I asked a
friend who is a Greek scholar to help me understand the difference between *conform* and *transform*.

He told me the word translated *conform* referred to the outward form. For example, my outward form at age twenty was
quite different from what I'll look like at age seventy. The body
changes, but it was more than that. He said the Greek word carried the idea of the changes we make according to the fashion—
what was in vogue at the time—much like the way our culture
goes today. One year, skirt hems are above the ankle; another
year, above the knee. Those things are constantly changing.

The word Paul used for being *transformed* from the world

refers to the essential part of ourselves—the part that doesn't change. He was saying that if we want to worship and serve God, we must undergo a change—but not only of our outward form. The change must be inward, and it involves our personality, our mind, and our essential being.

Outward fashions may change, but inner purity is always in style.

Romans 12:1, the verse that starts this chapter, exhorts us to present ourselves to God as a living a sacrifice. Only Christians can do that. His words are not about *becoming* believers, but they are about *living as* believers. This scripture challenges us to present all of our members to God for His use. That means our minds, mouths, wills, emotions, eyes, ears, hands, feet, et cetera.

I have to admit that for many years, I was active in the church, and I had accepted Jesus as my Savior. I knew I'd go to heaven, but I am not sure my daily witness would have encouraged anyone else to make a commitment to Jesus Christ. I had no victory, and I wasn't even aware for a long time that I needed victory. I guess I thought life was being miserable all week and going to church on Sunday, hoping God would forgive me for not being a good person.

God changed that for me. He helped me understand through His Word that He not only sent Jesus to die for us so we could go to heaven, but also so we could live victoriously right here on earth. We are more than conquerors (see Romans 8:37), and our life should include righteousness, peace, and joy in the Holy Spirit (see Romans 14:17).

If we want to see God's perfect will proven in our lives, we can—but we have to have our minds transformed. We have to think different thoughts and look at life differently. We have to have disciplined minds. We must begin to think in agreement with God's Word and not the devil's lies.

Although God has a different plan for each one of us, one thing is the same: We are to have minds that are inwardly transformed. If our minds are transformed by the Holy Spirit, we will act differently. I know I did. Church became a place for me to celebrate and to learn with my brothers and sisters in the faith. I began to understand worship, and I became a participant rather than someone who simply went through the motions.

Does your life need to be transformed? Start by being willing to think right thoughts, and then you'll see the change in yourself . . . and so will others around you.

Holy Spirit of God, please help me live a life that's transformed by the renewing of my mind. Help me live a life that shows Your perfect will, not only to me but also to the world. I ask this through Your Son, Jesus Christ. Amen.

36

Think About What You Are Thinking About

Whatever is true, whatever is worthy of reverence and is honorable and seemly, whatever is just, whatever is pure, whatever is lovely and lovable, whatever is kind and winsome and gracious, if there is any virtue and excellence, if there is anything worthy of praise, think on and weigh and take account of these things [fix your minds on them].
—Philippians 4:8b

Some people are very unhappy, and they have been that way so long that they no longer realize there is another option. I can well remember being like that. I blamed my unhappiness on the way others behaved. I thought my husband and children caused me the most unhappiness. If they would change and just be a little more sensitive to my needs, I knew I'd feel better. If they would help around the house more, volunteer to run errands, or just ask how I was doing, I knew I'd be happy. Of course, I never said anything to them. *If they were sensitive and caring,* I thought, *they would be able to see how they could help me and make my life easier.*

I did pray about it, and I often told God how much happier I would be if they cooperated more, but they didn't change.

One day, God spoke to me—but not with the words I wanted to hear. He said, *Think about what you are thinking about.* I had no idea what God meant. In fact, the words didn't make sense. How could I think about what I was thinking about?

Then I realized the truth. My mind raced from one thought to another. That was bad enough, but worse, my thoughts centered around myself and my needs. I had thought that if *they—the other people in my life*—changed, I would be happy. I finally reluctantly admitted that even if they changed, I'd find something else to be unhappy about. I was just unhappy and didn't need any particular reason. It was first one thing and then another.

As I pondered my condition, I thought of Philippians 4:8, where Paul presented a list of the kind of things we need to focus on. If God did not want me to think about the things I was thinking about, I first needed to know what I *should* think about. I soon realized I had a lot to learn. Although I had been attending church for years, I could not remember anyone ever telling me how important my thoughts were to God and to my quality of life.

If we concentrate our thoughts on good things—the kind of things Paul mentioned in that verse—we will be built up. We will grow spiritually and become strong in the Lord.

As I continued to meditate on God's message, I realized how my thoughts affected my attitude—and this is true of all of us. God tells us to do things that are for our good. He wants us to be happy and fulfilled. If we want happiness and fulfillment, we must find it God's way. If we're full of wrong thoughts, we're miserable. That's not a theory—that's spoken from my own experience and is found in God's Word. I've also learned that when we're miserable, we usually end up making others around us miserable, too.

Since those days, I've made it a practice to take a regular inventory of my thoughts. I review the way I think. *What have I been thinking about?* I ask myself.

I stress this because—as I learned from my own experience—Satan deceives us into thinking that the source of our misery or pain is other people or sometimes our situations. He tries not to let us face the fact that our own thoughts are the source of our unhappiness. I would venture to say that it is practically impossible to be happy while maintaining negative, critical, depressing thoughts.

We need to overcome Satan in this area of the battle for our thoughts, and God will help us if we ask Him to.

Dear Lord Jesus, I have determined to think about the things I have been thinking about. I admit that my thoughts are the source of any unhappiness that I experience and not other people. I also know that the source of my victory is in You, and in Your name, I ask You to give me greater victory as I monitor my thoughts through the help of the Holy Spirit. Amen.

37

The Condition of Our Minds

But we have the mind of Christ (the Messiah) and do hold the thoughts (feelings and purposes) of His heart.
—1 CORINTHIANS 2:16 (B)

I reached the curb in front of the airport, where my friend would pick me up. I was calm and relaxed and thought of the great conversation we would have. To my surprise, she wasn't there yet. That was odd because she's the kind of person who is never late for anything. I remained calm and peaceful. I spotted what I thought was her car and took a step forward, but the car went past me, and there was a stranger in it.

Not more than three minutes had passed, but I realized I was anxious and worried. What had happened to her? Had she been in an accident? Did she forget me? From calmness to anxiety in less than three minutes, and nothing had changed—nothing except my mind. Worried thoughts struggled inside me.

I pulled out my cell phone and started to dial, when I heard a car honking, as she pulled up to the curb. My mind shifted once again to calmness, even joyfulness. How quickly my emotions had shifted in that short period of time.

My mind had quickly changed when my circumstances did. Sometimes I find it easy to hear God speak . . . and to believe without any difficulty. Yet at other times, worry and anxiety push their way into my mind. The Bible says we are to walk by faith and not by sight, but that day at the airport, I was definitely being led by what I saw. When we worry, we are not walking in faith and trusting God.

For a long period of my life, I had a critical, suspicious, and judgmental mind. That may seem normal for many nonbelievers, but I was a Christian. I was going along with the same thinking and mindset that I had known for years. It was normal to me—it was just the way I was. For years, I had no awareness that my wrong thinking was causing any problems.

Because no one had taught me, I didn't know I could do anything to change my thought life. It simply had not occurred to me. No one had taught me about the proper condition for the believer's mind. God offers us a new way to think and a new way to live.

God has called us to renew our minds (see Romans 12:2). For most of us, it is an ongoing process. We don't control our thinking all at one time.

One day I read 1 Corinthians 2:16, where Paul says we have the mind of Christ. What could he have meant? I pondered that verse for days. I concluded that for us to have the mind of Christ doesn't mean we're sinless or perfect. It does mean we begin to think the way Christ thinks. If we have His mind, we think on those things that are good and honorable and loving.

I confessed to God how many times my mind had focused on the ugly, the mean, and the harsh.

In 1 Corinthians 2:14, Paul wrote, "But the natural, non-spiritual man does not accept or welcome or admit into his heart the gifts and teachings and revelations of the Spirit of God, for they are folly (meaningless nonsense) to him . . . because they are spiritually discerned and estimated and appreciated. . . ." *Yes,* I thought, *that's exactly how it works. The natural mind—even that of the Christians whose minds are tampered with by Satan—doesn't grasp what God is doing. Those things seem foolish.*

We must remind ourselves that we have Christ's mind—we have the ability to think loving and caring thoughts. We can defeat Satan's attacks.

Holy God, I want to live with the mind of Christ. I ask You to enable me to think positive, loving, caring thoughts about myself and about others. Help me to see and think on the good things in life and not the bad. I ask this in Jesus' name. Amen.

38

My Normal Mind

I do not cease to give thanks for you, making mention of you in my prayers. [For I always pray to] the God of our Lord Jesus Christ, the Father of glory, that He may grant you a spirit of wisdom and revelation [of insight into mysteries and secrets] in the [deep and intimate] knowledge of Him, by having the eyes of your heart flooded with light, so that you can know and understand the hope to which He has called you, and how rich is His glorious inheritance in the saints (His set-apart ones).

—Ephesians 1:16–18

This section in Ephesians is difficult for many of us to understand. What does Paul mean by "the eyes of your heart flooded with light" (v. 18)? I believe he is referring to the mind, because that's what needs enlightenment. It is with the mind that we grasp God's truths and hold to them.

Too many of us have difficulty being "flooded with light" because we are distracted with too many other things. The apostle prays for us to have what I call a normal mind—a mind that's open to the Holy Spirit's work—so that we may follow God's plan and live enriched lives.

One way to think about the idea of a normal mind is to look at two of Jesus' friends, Mary and Martha. Most people know the story of the sisters and the visit Jesus made to their home in Bethany. Martha scurried around, making certain that everything in their home was exactly right, while Mary sat down to listen to Jesus. Luke says Martha "was distracted with much serving" (Luke 10:40), and she complained to Jesus that she needed her sister's help.

"Martha, Martha, you are anxious and troubled about many things" (v. 41), Jesus told her, and then He commended Mary for having chosen the "good portion."

As I thought about that incident, I realized it was more than Martha being distracted. I'm sure her mind jumped around, making certain that everything was exactly right. The implication is that even if there had been nothing more to do, Martha wouldn't have stopped to sit at Jesus' feet. She was so caught up in busyness that her mind would have searched for something else to do.

The Marthas seem to be in control of our world, don't they? They are the ones who get things done. When they're not accomplishing their own goals, they seem to be telling others what they should do. In today's world of "multi-tasking," the Marthas seem to get the awards and the accolades. Some people are busy all the time. They wear their busyness like a badge, as if that makes them more important.

Their busyness can easily distract them from developing a solid relationship with God. They're the ones who often lack depth of peace and rarely know spiritual contentment. That is, they don't have what God considers a normal mind. It is not in the condition He would like it to be in.

People who are excessively busy cannot even sleep when they lie down at night. They are either mentally going over the day's activities or making mental lists of the tasks for the next day.

This isn't the lifestyle Jesus calls us to. As believers, we are spiritual beings, but we're also natural. The natural doesn't understand the spiritual and constantly fights that part of our nature. The Bible makes it clear that the mind and the spirit work together. That's the principle I call "the mind aiding the spirit."

For the mind to aid the spirit, we must learn to pull back from all the distractions around us. There will always be demands on our time and energy, and we can always find plenty to do. But if we want to live with the mind of Christ, the one that should be normal for Christians, it means we must learn to imitate Mary. Despite all the clamor and activities going on around her, she was able to sit, relax, and listen to the voice of the Master. That's how the mind is supposed to work. It should be quiet and under the control of the Spirit. However, we often find that our minds are so set in a wrong direction that they actually hinder the Spirit from helping us, as they should be free to do.

If you realize from this devotion that your mind has been behaving abnormally, ask God to forgive you and teach you what a normal mind is in His kingdom.

Dear God in heaven, distractions constantly come at me. When I try to pause and focus on You, my mind seems to be filled with dozens of things I need to do. I realize that I truly need only one thing—to focus on You. Please help me push away every distraction and noise so I can hear only Your voice that says, "Come unto Me, and I will give you rest." Amen.

39

Still, Small Voice

And He said, Go out and stand on the mount before the Lord.
And behold, the Lord passed by, and a great and strong wind
rent the mountains and broke in pieces the rocks before the
Lord, but the Lord was not in the wind; and after the wind an
earthquake, but the Lord was not in the earthquake; and after
the earthquake a fire, but the Lord was not in the fire; and after
the fire [a sound of gentle stillness and] a still, small voice.
—1 Kings 19:11–12

Someone once told me of a one-act play with three charac-
ters—a father, a mother, and a son who had just returned
from Viet Nam—who are sitting at a table to talk. The play
lasts thirty minutes, and they all get their chance to talk.
There's only one problem: No one listens to the others.

The father is about to lose his job. The mother had once
held just about every office in their church, and now younger
women are pushing her aside. The son struggles with his
faith. He had gone to war, seen chaos and death, and now is
bewildered about life.

At the end of the play, the son stands and heads toward the

door. "You haven't heard a word I've said," is his parting re-
mark, as he walks out of the room.

The parents look at each other, and the mother asks,
"What did he mean?"

What the parents didn't get—and the audience obviously
does—is that the son struggles to believe in a loving, caring
God. Every time he tries to explain, one of the parents interrupts with something they want to say. The soldier needed to
hear from God. Hoping his mother or father would be the
channel through which God would speak, he went to them.
However, they were not available for God to use because they
were not quiet enough to hear Him. All three of them were so
distraught and noisy that they all left the same way they
came. What might have happened had they really listened to
one another, and then quietly prayed and waited on God? I
am sure the outcome would have been very different and
much more rewarding.

In the opening scripture, I quoted part of the story of Elijah to make this point clear. That deeply committed prophet
had defied the wicked King Ahab and Queen Jezebel for
years. The big moment came on Mount Carmel when Elijah
destroyed 450 prophets of Baal. Later, when Queen Jezebel
threatened to kill him, he ran away, apparently in terror.

He must have been worn out by the powerful events. Then
suddenly the man was alone, with no crowds, no one trying
to kill him, and no one to talk to. Just before the two verses
mentioned above, Elijah had gone into a cave to hide out.
When God asked him what he was doing there, he spoke of

his zeal for God. Then he told God that the children of Israel had gone astray, killing prophets, "And I, I only, am left; and they seek my life, to take it away" (v. 10).

God brought strong winds, falling rocks, an earthquake, and fire. I think that was the way Elijah expected God to appear—in the miraculous and powerful. But the writer tells us God wasn't in those things.

This is really the spiritual principle of God at work. We can find the devil in the noise and the shouts. We can find the devil with big attractions to lead us astray. But God likes to speak in the still, small voice—the voice that not everyone will hear—the voice that only the committed will listen for.

As long as Elijah sought the dramatic, he wouldn't hear God. But when he pulled back and listened for the inner voice, the soft, non-demanding voice of the Holy Spirit, Elijah could communicate with God.

What kind of voice from God are you listening for? Will you recognize the still, small voice when you hear it? Do you take time to be quiet and just listen? If not, there is no better time to begin than right now.

Wise God, like Elijah and many others, I often look for the loud, the exciting, and the showy. I know that You sometimes use healings and miracles, but I ask You to help me listen most of all in the soft stillness for the quiet ways in which You speak. In Jesus' name, I pray. Amen.

40

Spiritual Praying

Then what am I to do? I will pray with my spirit [by the Holy Spirit that is within me], but I will also pray [intelligently] with my mind and understanding; I will sing with my spirit [by the Holy Spirit that is within me], but I will sing [intelligently] with my mind and understanding also.

—1 Corinthians 14:15

Earlier I referred to "the mind aiding the spirit." For many people, this is a difficult concept to grasp. I understand what Paul meant because it's something I've learned to use in my own spiritual growth.

For example, one morning I set aside my usual time for prayer. I began to pray, but my prayers felt flat—nothing energized them—and there was no help from my spirit. As I struggled, I reminded myself that I had made myself available to God, and I wanted the Spirit to use me to change lives.

I continued to pray but nothing changed. This had happened before, so I wasn't discouraged. I kept on praying and telling God the things about which I was concerned. After several minutes, a powerful energy took hold of me. I *knew* I had touched the area where the Holy Spirit wanted me to pray. This became more than my concern—this was God's concern.

I began by praying out of my mind—about things that I knew of and thought needed prayer. I was praying in English because that is my normal language, and I understood what I was saying. But when the energizing power of the Spirit came, without any conscious thought, I began to pray with my prayer language, or what many of us refer to as an unknown tongue.

Paul was our example and teacher in this area. He said he knew how to pray with the Spirit, and he knew how to pray with the understanding. This may not make sense to everyone—and it certainly can confuse people at first. However, I encourage you not to reject a gift of God that is available to you merely because you have not experienced it and don't understand it. Be open to God, and ask Him to teach you about praying in other tongues.

Think of it this way. God calls us to prayer. That's our joy as well as our responsibility. Sometimes when we talk to God, we hardly know what to say. We pray, but our words feel inadequate. It's as if there is a depth to our burdens that transcends words. Something is going on that's so strong within us—so overwhelming—we have no words to speak. To use English feels utterly useless. No matter what we say to God out of our own minds (understanding), we feel we have not broken through and obtained a victory.

Then comes what I call a prayer release. I speak in words I don't understand—words that are beyond the grasp of my human mind—and yet my spirit "understands," or bears witness that my prayers are correct and are getting the job done.

The best biblical reference I can give for this experience is Acts 2, which tells the story of Pentecost. The disciples prayed in an upper room while Jews came from all over the world to the city of Jerusalem. The 120 people in that room were so filled with the Holy Spirit that they burst out speaking in unknown languages—unknown to them. But the visitors heard them, "And when this sound was heard, the multitude came together and they were astonished and bewildered, because each one heard them [the apostles] speaking in his own [particular] dialect" (Acts 2:6).

The apostle Paul thanked God that he spoke in tongues, and he also said that nobody should forbid anyone to do so. There has been a great deal of division in the church over the issue of speaking in tongues, but I encourage you to go straight to your Bible and see what the Word of God says about it. Don't have a closed mind to any of the precious gifts of the Holy Spirit. We need all the supernatural help we can get to help us live our lives victoriously.

Some people teach that the gift of speaking in tongues went away with the early church, but there are millions of people worldwide who speak in tongues today. Those who speak in other tongues are certainly no better, nor are they more spiritual than those who do not speak in tongues, but once again, I encourage you to seek God for yourself in this area, so your prayers can be as powerful as possible.

When we pray in the Spirit, our minds and our spirits work together. Our minds yield to our spirits, and we are praying the perfect prayer that God desires.

———————

Holy Spirit, I desire all the supernatural gifts You have made available. I need all the help I can get to enable me to live victoriously. I want to pray powerful prayers that are led by the Holy Spirit. I know You hear and answer the prayers I pray in my known language, but I am open to receiving the gift of an unknown language that will enable me to speak secrets and mysteries unto You. I trust You, Jesus, to lead me in the right direction. Amen.

41

God's Vision for You

For I know the thoughts and plans that I have for you, says the Lord, thoughts and plans for welfare and peace and not for evil, to give you hope in your final outcome.
—JEREMIAH 29:11

God's plan for the people of the nation of Israel was only for their good. Yet they wandered around in the wilderness for forty years on what was actually an eleven-day journey. Why? Was it their enemies, their circumstances, the trials along the way, or something entirely different that prevented them from arriving at their destination in a timely manner?

God called the children of Israel out of bondage in Egypt to go to the land He had promised to give them as a perpetual inheritance—a land that flowed with milk and honey and every good thing they could imagine—a land in which there would be no shortage of anything they needed—a land of prosperity in every realm of their existence.

But the Israelites had no positive vision for their lives—no dreams. They knew where they came from, but they did not know where they were going. Everything was based on what they had seen in the past or what they could presently see. They did not know how to see with "the eye of faith."

We really shouldn't view the Israelites with astonishment, because most of us do the same thing they did. We keep dealing with the same problems over and over again. The disappointing result is that it takes us years to experience victory over something that could have and should have been dealt with quickly.

I come from a background of abuse. My childhood was filled with fear and torment, and my personality was a mess! I built up walls of protection to keep people from hurting me, not realizing that while I was locking others out, I was also locking myself in. I was filled with fear, and believed that the only way I could face life was to be *in control* so no one could hurt me.

As a young adult trying to live for Christ and follow the Christian lifestyle, I knew where I had come from, but I did not know where I was going. I felt that my future would always be marred by my past. I thought, *How could anyone with a past like mine ever be all right? It's impossible!*

But Jesus had a different plan. He said, "The Spirit of the Lord [is] upon Me . . . to preach the good news (the Gospel) to the poor; He has sent Me to announce release to the captives and recovery of sight to the blind, to send forth as delivered those who are oppressed [who are downtrodden, bruised, crushed, and broken down by calamity]" (Luke 4:18).

Jesus came to open the prison doors and set the captives free—and that included me. However, I did not make any progress until I started to believe that I really *could* be set free.

I had to get rid of my negative thinking and replace it with a positive vision for my life. I had to believe that neither my past nor my present could determine my future. Only then could Jesus free me from the bondage of my past—and free me, He did. What a marvelous miracle!

You may have had a miserable past; you may even be in current circumstances that are very negative and depressing. You may be facing situations that are so bad it seems you have no real reason to hope. But I say to you boldly: *Your future is not determined by your past or your present!*

Most of the generation the Lord called out of Egypt never entered into the Promised Land. Instead, they died in the wilderness. To me, this is one of the saddest things that can happen to a child of God—to have so much available and yet never be able to enjoy any of it.

Start believing that God's Word is true. Mark 9:23 assures you that with God *all* things are possible. Because you serve a God who created everything you see out of the unseen realm (see Hebrews 11:3), you can give Him your nothingness and watch Him go to work on your behalf. All you have to do is have faith in Him and believe His Word—He will do the rest!

Dear Father, I thank You for loving me and having a vision—a good plan—for my life. I pray that You will help me overcome any negative thoughts of problems, past or present, that come against my mind, and make my life what You want it to be. Amen.

42

The Peaceful Mind

You will guard him and keep him in perfect and constant peace whose mind [both its inclination and its character] is stayed on You, because he commits himself to You, leans on You, and hopes confidently in You.

—Isaiah 26:3

What is it about nighttime that makes us more vulnerable to satanic attack? Is it because daylight is gone and it's dark? Is there some kind of association between evil and the dark hours of night? We are usually able to cope with whatever happens to us during the day, but sometimes it's a different story at night.

My theory is that by evening, most of us are tired and weary, and we just want to lie down, close our eyes, and drift into peaceful sleep. That is one of Satan's favorite times to engage us in the battle for our minds. He knows that when we are exhausted and sleepy, we are not as resistant to his attacks. And just as we are about to drop off to sleep, he makes his move.

If we recognize that we're more susceptible to the attack of the enemy at night, we can take steps to be better prepared to stand against him. Some of my friends tell me that they find it helps to meditate on scriptures such as Philippians 4:8, which tells us to think on good things—things that are true, honorable, just, pure, lovely, and excellent. Or they claim the promise of Isaiah 26:3: "You will guard him and keep him in perfect and constant peace whose mind [both its inclination and its character] is stayed on You. . . ." These words from the Bible enable us to remain vigilant even in the dark hours of night. By using the Word of God, we can defeat every onslaught of the enemy—even in our weakest hours.

But if we have not armed ourselves with the Word and spent some time in prayer, we will fall for Satan's plan when he brings to mind some troublesome event of the day, and asks, "Why did you say that? How could you have been so insensitive?"

He takes advantage of us when he knows we are weak and the most vulnerable to his influence. His goal is to disturb our thoughts and rob us of the peaceful rest that our bodies need. One of his tricks is to cause us to focus on the problems of the day, suggesting that we must immediately—in the middle of the night—determine the best way to settle the issue.

I experienced nights like this years ago, and I didn't always win the battle. But as a mature Christian, I now know how to fight the good fight of faith. Here's one thing I figured out a long time ago: It is not wise to make decisions in the middle of the night. There may be times when God demands an immediate surrender, and those are powerful moments in our lives. But most decisions can wait until the next day.

Perhaps we spoke hastily or didn't respond kindly to someone's need. The issues are often little things that we probably could have handled better. But as Satan wages his battle in the dark of night, those little things seem to take on importance and urgency—so much so that we believe we will never sleep unless we settle the issue *immediately*.

When Satan tries to pull that nighttime trick on me, I've learned to say, "I'll deal with this issue in the morning, when the sun is shining. After I've rested, I can cope." I've also learned that I can say, "Lord, I surrender this to You. Give me Your rest, Your peace, and help me to make the right decision in the morning." That works for me!

Holy Spirit, thank You for being with me, for protecting me, and for guiding my life. When I face those dark nights and the enemy tries to attack my mind, protect me. I trust You and ask You to keep me in Your perfect peace. Amen.

43

A Wandering, Wondering Mind

Wherefore gird up the loins of your mind, be sober, and hope to the end for the grace that is to be brought unto you at the revelation of Jesus Christ.

—1 PETER 1:13 KJV

In the days when Peter wrote these words, men wore long, flowing robes that hindered fast progress or strenuous action. They wore broad belts (or girdles) about their waists, and when they wanted to move into action, they "girded up their loins"—that is, they shortened their robes by pulling them up inside their belts. That term is similar to what we mean when we say, "Roll up your sleeves." Peter's words here are a serious call to action—a reminder that when we lose our focus, it is time for us to do some serious thinking.

I've already talked about how staying too busy can result in an abnormal mind as opposed to a normal mind. Now I want to point out that another way the devil attacks your normal mind is by causing your thoughts to wander. It's a mental attack. If you do not discipline your mind to remain focused on what is important, the devil will cause it to wander aimlessly to other things.

When this inability to concentrate goes on for a while, you may begin to wonder if there is something wrong with your mind. What you often fail to realize is that when you've allowed your mind to wander for so long, you're hardly aware that it's taking place.

In some cases, there may be physical causes for not being able to concentrate, such as anemia or certain B-vitamin deficiencies. You may not be eating properly. Or you may have become excessively fatigued. It's a good idea to consider all the potential causes as you search for a solution. I've learned that when I'm excessively tired, Satan tries to attack my mind because he knows it's more difficult for me to resist him during those times.

Sometimes a lack of concentration creates a lack of comprehension. Perhaps as you are reading the Bible, you find yourself hurrying to get through so you can do something else. Out of a sense of duty, you are determined to finish reading a chapter—and you do. But when you are finished, you can't recall anything you have read. Your eyes scanned the pages, but your mind was engaged somewhere else.

Perhaps you have even experienced this battle for your mind in church. You attend regularly—and the devil can't always stop that—but he *can* cause your mind to start wandering during the sermon. Have you ever been fully engrossed in listening to a sermon, and then you suddenly realize that your mind has wandered and you have no idea what was said?

If the devil can rob you of the benefits of reading the Bible and hearing God's Word at church, he has won some major skirmishes in the battle for your mind. This is why Peter tells us to "gird up the loins of our minds." You must take action by confronting your wandering mind and disciplining it to focus on what's important.

In conversation, I used to fake it when I realized my mind had wandered. Now I deal with it honestly by asking, "Would you please back up and repeat that? I let my mind wander off, and I didn't hear a thing you said." This kind of behavior not only interrupts the plan of the enemy but also brings victory over the problem.

It's not easy to discipline your mind when it has been allowed to wander aimlessly, but you can do it. When you discover that your thoughts have wandered, you must exercise discipline and make the necessary corrections. The devil would like to convince you that you can't help yourself, but when you consistently come against his bid for your mind, he is defeated, and you have won another battle.

Holy Spirit, I realize how quickly Satan distracts me and then capitalizes on my wandering mind. Forgive me for allowing him to lead me astray. I thank You for giving me a good, clear mind, and in the name of Jesus, I ask You to help me overcome every temptation to lose my focus. Amen.

44

A Wondering Mind

In the morning, when they were passing along, they noticed that the fig tree was withered [completely] away to its roots. And Peter remembered and said to Him, Master, look! The fig tree which You doomed has withered away! And Jesus, replying, said to them, Have faith in God [constantly]. Truly I tell you, whoever says to this mountain, Be lifted up and thrown into the sea! and does not doubt at all in his heart but believes that what he says will take place, it will be done for him. For this reason I am telling you, whatever you ask for in prayer, believe (trust and be confident) that it is granted to you, and you will [get it].

—MARK 11:20–24

When you say the words, "I wonder," they sound innocent and honest. They also represent the way we avoid certainty in making decisions.

Suppose you're the CEO of a business. Every day twenty people come to your office and ask you to make decisions. Yours is the final answer on everything that goes on in the corporation. Instead of giving decisive answers, you rub your chin, stare out the window, and say, "I wonder. I wonder what we should do about that?"

An indecisive CEO wouldn't stay in that position very long. The position is much too important to the overall success and wellbeing of the organization and all who are associated with it. You are not in that position to wonder—you're there to act.

Too many of us forget that this is the way it is with the Christian life, as well. Too often, instead of choosing what we need to do, we avoid facing the situation and say, "I wonder."

I know because I've done it. In times past, when I've been invited to a party or to be the featured speaker at a banquet, I've said, "I wonder what I should wear." It's easy for me to waste a lot of time looking through my closet, considering the color and style, as I try to choose just the right outfit for a particular occasion.

This may seem like such a small thing—and it really is. The problem, however, is that if we allow enough of these "wonderings" in our lives, we not only fail to accomplish the things we need to do, but wondering becomes the normal way our minds function. Being indecisive keeps us from moving forward and can eventually defeat us.

In the verses quoted earlier, the incident started with a fig tree that wasn't bearing fruit. The disciples could have wasted time wondering about the particulars of why the tree didn't bear fruit. They could have wondered if it hadn't received enough sunlight or water. They might have wondered why the owner hadn't cut it down since it wasn't productive. But wasting time wondering really wasn't necessary.

When Jesus spoke and doomed the tree, He put a stop to any mental speculation. He used the incident as an object lesson for the disciples, encouraging them to believe. He wanted them to understand that if they truly believed, they could have whatever they asked of Him.

Sometimes God's people are reluctant to ask boldly for big things. But Jesus has given us permission to step out in faith and ask boldly. And yet some still waste time just wondering. They wonder what it would be like if God would give them a better job. They wonder what it would be like if God would give them a larger house.

I can tell you that wondering is a waste of time. So stop wondering and start acting! That's one of the most important things I've learned about the wondering mind. Rather than wondering what I should wear to a banquet, I look at my clothes and I decide. God gave me the ability to make wise choices, so I can just do it instead of wasting my time wondering.

Wondering and indecision can become strongholds in our minds that can leave us feeling confused, insecure, and ineffective. But that's not God's plan. He wants us to overcome the wondering thoughts by believing and then receiving the answer to our prayers from God, by faith.

Notice that Jesus did not say, "Whatever things you wonder when you pray, you will have." Instead, He said, "Whatever you ask for in prayer, believe (trust and be confident) that it is granted to you, and you will [get it]."

Lord Jesus, help me to overcome any wondering tendencies that keep me from moving forward in Your good plan. In Your name, I ask You to help me reach out in faith, boldly asking for what I need. Then help me to believe it and receive it. Amen.

45

A Confused Mind

If any of you is deficient in wisdom, let him ask of the giving God [Who gives] to everyone liberally and ungrudgingly, without reproaching or faultfinding, and it will be given him. Only it must be in faith that he asks with no wavering (no hesitating, no doubting). For the one who wavers (hesitates, doubts) is like the billowing surge out at sea that is blown hither and thither and tossed by the wind. For truly, let not such a person imagine that he will receive anything [he asks for] from the Lord, [for being as he is] a man of two minds (hesitating, dubious, irresolute), [he is] unstable and unreliable and uncertain about everything [he thinks, feels, decides].

—James 1:5–8

My friend Eva received a summons for jury duty in a robbery trial. For two days, twelve citizens listened to the prosecuting attorney as he presented evidence to indicate that the accused had broken into a home and stolen many items. Eva was ready to convict him.

On the third day, the defense attorney presented the other side of the picture. The more Eva listened, the more confused she became. What had seemed very obvious at first now seemed ambiguous and contradictory.

Although the jury did convict the man, Eva said she struggled over making the right decision. Each attorney, when he was speaking, had seemed to be the most convincing.

Many Christians live much the same way day to day. They have become what James calls double-minded. They're sure of one thing until something else happens, and then they flip-flop to the opposite opinion.

In their double-mindedness, they flit from one opinion to the other. They're sure they know what to do, and then they switch again. The moment they feel sure they have made the decision they plan to stick with, they begin to wonder if it was the correct one. They continually doubt and question their reasoning.

This kind of behavior is not the same as being open-minded. To be open-minded means we're willing to hear all sides of an issue—like jurors should be at a trial. But eventually we have to sort through the evidence or the circumstances in life and say, "This is what I'm going to do."

That sounds good, but too many people have trouble being decisive. "What if I make a mistake?" they ask. "What If I choose the wrong thing?" Those are legitimate questions, but they are not meant to paralyze God's people and prevent them from acting. Too often, these are tools that Satan uses to distract and prevent Christians from taking action.

I'm an expert on this. For many years, I was that double-minded person James wrote about. I didn't like being that way. It took so much energy to keep rethinking the same problems. But I was so afraid of making a mistake that I didn't know how to make good decisions. It took a long time before I realized that the devil had declared war against me, and that my mind was his personal battlefield. At that moment of awareness, I felt totally confused about everything, and I didn't understand why.

So many of God's people are living exactly where I was then. They're reasonable people. That is, they have the ability to figure out causes and relationships and reasons. They sincerely try to understand all the implications of a situation and then find the most sensible or logical solution by putting their reasoning ability to work.

Too often, this is where Satan sneaks in and steals the will of God from them. God may speak to them about doing a certain thing, and it may not always seem to be the most sensible course of action. This presents an opportunity for the devil to cause them to question—to become double-minded.

For example, sometimes I sense that God wants me to bless people by giving to them—often an item of jewelry or clothing. On occasion, God wants me to give away a new and fairly expensive dress that I've never worn. It doesn't make sense when I go through the natural reasoning process, but when I open myself to the Spirit of God, I have the assurance that it is the right thing to do.

God's Spirit is always available to free you from natural

reasoning that leaves you confused. Ask of the One who gives wisdom liberally, and He will free you of being indecisive and double-minded.

Dear Father, in the past, I've been double-minded and confused, giving Satan an advantage over me. Please forgive me. I ask You now, in faith, to give me the necessary wisdom to overcome all of Satan's confusion. In Jesus' name, I pray. Amen.

46

Just Obey

But the natural, nonspiritual man does not accept or welcome or admit into his heart the gifts and teachings and revelations of the Spirit of God, for they are folly (meaningless nonsense) to him; and he is incapable of knowing them (of progressively recognizing, understanding, and becoming better acquainted with them) because they are spiritually discerned and estimated and appreciated.

—1 CORINTHIANS 2:14

Many non-Christians don't really understand the gospel. This isn't a new thing that is unique to our day. When Paul wrote to the Corinthians, he pointed out that the Greeks thought it was foolish. And to the natural mind, it is. God sent Jesus, the sinless One, to earth for the express purpose of dying for wicked, sinful people. To unbelievers that is foolish. The natural man cannot understand the power of the gospel—it can only be "spiritually discerned."

This is just as true in daily living. Sometimes God speaks to us, and if we try to explain it to people who don't know Jesus, it doesn't make sense. For example, I remember one couple that went to Africa as missionaries. They had no denomination or large church behind them, providing support. They sold everything they owned, including their wedding rings.

"Their wedding rings?" a skeptical relative asked. "You mean God wouldn't provide for you, so you had to do it yourself?"

The wife smiled. "No, I think we had to decide if comfort and having things like everyone else was more important than serving Jesus." The couple never doubted they were doing the right thing, but it never made sense to the skeptical relative.

It is difficult for many people to hear God speak and to obey without question. But Jesus did just that—and not only on the cross. John 4 relates the story of Jesus and the Samaritan woman at the well. What most modern readers don't get is the introduction to the story: "It was necessary for Him to go through Samaria" (John 4:4). Jesus had been in Jerusalem, and He wanted to go north to Galilee. The country of the Samaritans was in between, but Jesus didn't have to take the route that passed that way. He could have taken another route and avoided going through Samaria. Most Jews avoided going through Samaria because they hated the Samaritans for mixing and marrying with people from other nations.

But Jesus went to Samaria, even though it wasn't what we would have called the normal or reasonable thing to do. He went because there was a woman—and eventually a whole village—that needed to hear the message that only He could deliver.

The natural people—those whose minds have not been

enlightened by the Holy Spirit—scoff at us. What we do doesn't always make sense to them. But then, who says our actions have to make sense? The biblical principle is that the natural or carnal mind doesn't understand spiritual things. Too often, a thought comes to us that we push aside, saying, *This doesn't make any sense,* and we actually ignore divine guidance. It's true, of course, that the devil can flood our minds with wild thoughts, but if we pray and open ourselves to the Spirit, we soon know the difference.

Consider the story of Peter who had fished all night and caught nothing. Jesus, a carpenter, came along and told him, a professional fisherman, "Put out into the deep [water], and lower your nets for a haul" (Luke 5:4).

Peter reasoned with Jesus, reminding Him that they had worked all night and caught nothing. But to his credit, Peter, exhausted from a long and unsuccessful night's work, heard the Lord. I'll say it again, Peter *heard* the Lord and said, "But on the ground of Your word, I will lower the nets [again]" (v. 5). And Peter was not disappointed. They caught so many fish that the nets almost broke.

This is an important principle of obedience that we must grasp: obey instead of reasoning. Or as one of my friends calls it, "The Nevertheless Principle." She says that sometimes she feels God leading her to do things that don't always make a lot of sense. When she hears herself expressing that sentiment, she quickly adds, "Nevertheless." Then she obeys.

That is really all God asks of us: to obey instead of reasoning.

Wise and wonderful God, sometimes things don't make sense to me, but nevertheless, I want to be in Your will. Help me to develop spiritual discernment, and don't let me miss a divine opportunity to serve You. Teach me to trust You more, and help me to obey You quickly instead of trying to reason things out. Thank You for hearing me today. Amen.

47

Doing the Word

But be doers of the Word [obey the message], and not merely listeners to it, betraying yourselves [into deception by reasoning contrary to the Truth].
—JAMES 1:22

As a Christian, for a long time I didn't understand that believers could know what God wanted them to do and then deliberately say no. I'm not talking about those who turn their backs on Jesus and want nothing to do with His salvation. I'm talking about those who disobey in the seemingly little things and don't seem to be troubled by doing so.

In verses 23 and 24, James went on to say that if we only listen to the Word, but don't obey it, it's like looking at our reflection in a mirror and then going away and forgetting what we saw. But a doer of the Word, he says, is like one "who looks carefully into the faultless law, the [law] of liberty, and is faithful to it and perseveres in looking into it, being not a heedless listener who forgets but an active doer [who obeys], he shall be blessed in his doing (his life of obedience)" (v. 25).

Whenever Christians are faced with God's Word, and it calls them to action but they refuse to obey, their own human reasoning is often the cause. They have deceived themselves into believing something other than the truth. It's as if they think they are smarter than God.

I've met people who seem to think that God always wants them to feel good, and if something happens to make them feel bad, they don't believe it is God's will for them. Or they dismiss what they read in the Bible by saying, "That doesn't make sense."

One woman, referring to Paul's instruction to "be unceasing in prayer" (1 Thessalonians 5:17), said that verse kept coming to her every time she prayed.

"What do you think that means?" I asked her.

"Oh, I think it means that day in and day out, we are to pray when we feel a need or when we want something."

Her words shocked me. "What about fellowship with the Lord?" I asked. "Isn't that a good reason? Or maybe God just wants you to spend time reading His Word and praying about what you read."

"I have too many things to do," she said. "That's fine for people who like to sit and read and pray for hours every day, but that's not the way for me."

In our brief conversation, I learned that her decisions about obeying God's Word depended on whether or not it was convenient for her lifestyle. When she read things in the Bible that didn't fit with the way she lived, she explained it to herself in such a way that she convinced herself God didn't expect her to do *that*.

By contrast, I remember a very dignified woman who had

been a member of a traditional church most of her life. She often spoke of the noise and confusion in charismatic churches (although she had not been to one). Then she visited one of the services where I spoke and was transformed. "I couldn't believe that God would ask me to do something like clap my hands or sing loudly or even shout. But when I saw the joy on the faces of those in the congregation and heard you quote the Bible verse that commands us to clap our hands and shout, what else could I do? That was God speaking to me."

She had exactly the right attitude. She didn't try to reason it out or wonder why God commanded her to take that kind of action. She believed His Word and simply obeyed.

When the Bible speaks about obeying the Lord, it is not a suggestion. His Word doesn't ask, "Would you like to obey?" God *commands* us to take action by being a doer of His Word, and when we are obedient, He promises that we will be blessed.

Dear holy Father, I thank You for the instructions found in Your Word. I may not always like what I read, and sometimes it may be difficult to follow You without hesitating, but I know it is for my good. Please help me to be always obedient and to bring glory and honor to You. Amen.

48

Trust God

Lean on, trust in, and be confident in the Lord with all your heart and mind and do not rely on your own insight or understanding.

—Proverbs 3:5

The secret things belong unto the Lord our God, but the things which are revealed belong to us and to our children forever, that we may do all of the words of this law.

—Deuteronomy 29:29

I have heard many people say that reading the Bible is confusing. They say, "I have tried to read the Bible, but I don't understand what God is saying, and I end up feeling frustrated and confused."

In seeking God's guidance regarding this situation, I sensed Him saying, *People keep trying to figure out everything. Tell them to stop trying to reason and explain everything.* As the above verses point out, we cannot always rely on our understanding. There are some things that we are not meant to know or understand.

Moses understood this concept, and he explained to the children of Israel that there are "secret things" known only to God. He pointed out that when God revealed His will—making things clear—those were the words they should obey.

It really is that simple. Like the psalmist, we can say, "Give me understanding, that I may keep Your law; yes, I will observe it with my whole heart (Psalm 119:34). We must ask God to show us what to do, and then we must not question it when He reveals it to us.

Too often people try to reason things out, but that can be dangerous. When we start trying to figure out why God says or does something, our first mistake is thinking we're smart enough to understand the mind of God.

Reasoning can also move us in a particular direction that, although it may seem logical, may not be the will of God. A biblical account found in 1 Samuel is a good illustration of this point.

Saul, the first king of Israel, made a decision to offer sacrifices. As a part of the tribe of Benjamin, it was unlawful for him—even as the king—to offer sacrifices. The king and his army waited several days for Samuel, the high priest, to arrive. But eventually Saul grew impatient (or perhaps fearful) and offered sacrifices just before the holy man arrived. When Samuel rebuked Saul for doing such a thing, the king had what he believed to be a reasonable explanation: "I thought, The Philistines will come down now upon me to Gilgal, and I have not made supplication to the Lord. So I forced myself to offer a burnt offering" (1 Samuel 13:12).

Samuel rebuked the king, told him he had acted foolishly, and said the Lord was going to strip him of the kingdom.

That was Saul's mistake. He reasoned that it would be wise to sacrifice, and he didn't wait to hear from God.

The human mind likes logic, order, and reason. We like to deal with issues we can wrap our understanding around and come up with solutions that make sense to us. We have a tendency to think small because we are limited creatures, and we don't have the perspective to understand from God's point of view. We tend to put things in tiny, neat compartments in our minds, telling ourselves this must be right because it fits nicely there.

By contrast, we read the words of the apostle Paul: "I am speaking the truth in Christ. I am not lying; my conscience [enlightened and prompted] by the Holy Spirit bearing witness with me" (Romans 9:1). He was making the point that he was doing the right thing—not because he had figured it out or analyzed the situation, but because his actions bore witness in his spirit.

That's the attitude you need in your life. You need to depend on God to show you things in such a way that you know—with an inner certainty—that what has been revealed to your mind is correct. You must not allow yourself to reason with your mind, searching for logical solutions. Instead, you must say, "My trust is in the Lord, and whatever He tells me to do, I will obey."

Dear God, thank You for loving me more than I can even comprehend. In the name of Jesus Christ, I ask You to help me love and honor You so much that when You speak, I will have only one thought in my mind, and that is to obey. Amen.

49

Nothing But Christ

*For I resolved to know nothing (to be acquainted with
nothing, to make a display of the knowledge of nothing, and
to be conscious of nothing) among you except Jesus Christ
(the Messiah) and Him crucified. And I was in (passed into a
state of) weakness and fear (dread) and great trembling
[after I had come] among you. And my language and my
message were not set forth in persuasive (enticing and
plausible) words of wisdom, but they were in demonstration
of the [Holy] Spirit and power.*

—1 Corinthians 2:2–4

I've tried to imagine what it would have been like to go to
Corinth or other Greek cities at the time of Paul and try to
speak to those wise, brilliant thinkers. After studying every
parchment given to me, and gaining knowledge of all their
arguments, I would have prayed for God to help me overcome their objections.

We don't know what Paul did, but his answer is astound-
ing. Instead of going after them with great reasoning and
sharp logic, he went in exactly the opposite direction. He
stayed in Corinth a year and a half, and many came to Christ

because of him. Later, when he wrote 1 Corinthians, he said, "For I resolved to know nothing . . . among you except Jesus Christ (the Messiah) and Him crucified" (2:2). That's amazing. If any man had the ability to reason with those Greeks and could show them the fallacies of their logic, surely that man was Paul. But, being led by the Holy Spirit, he chose a defenseless presentation—to let God speak through him and touch the hearts of the people.

Now, centuries later, I appreciate his approach—although I didn't always feel this way. For a long time I wanted to explain and reason out everything, but when that didn't work, I ended up feeling miserable.

I've always been curious, always wanted to know, and always wanted to figure out the answer. Then God began to work in my life. He showed me that my constant drive to figure it out caused me confusion and prevented me from receiving many of the things He wanted me to have. He said, *You must lay aside carnal reasoning if you expect to have discernment.*

I didn't like loose ends, so I felt more secure when I figured things out. I wanted to be in control of every detail of every situation. When I didn't understand or was unable to figure things out, I felt out of control. And that was frightening to me. Something was wrong—I was troubled and had no peace of mind. Sometimes, frustrated and exhausted, I would just give up.

It was a long battle for me because I finally admitted something to myself (God knew it all along): I was *addicted* to reasoning. It was more than a tendency or desire to figure out things. It was a compulsion. I had to have answers—and had to have them right now. When God was finally able to convince me of my addiction, I was able to give it up.

It wasn't easy. Like people who withdraw from drugs or alcohol, I had withdrawal symptoms. I felt lost. Frightened. Alone. I had always depended on my ability to figure things out. Now, like Paul, I had to depend on God.

Too many people assume that relying only on God is something we do easily and naturally. It didn't work that way with me. But God was gracious and patient with me. It was as if He'd whisper, *You're not there yet, Joyce, but you're making progress. It's uncomfortable because you're learning a new way to live.*

God wants us to be victorious—and I knew that all along. Now I walk in greater victory than ever before—and I no longer try to reason out everything before I act.

Heavenly Father, thank You for being so patient with me and people like me who feel we must have all the answers before we can act or trust. In the name of Jesus, help me to simply trust in You, knowing that You will give me what is best for my life. Amen.

50

A Doubtful Mind

Elijah came near to all the people and said, How long will
you halt and limp between two opinions? If the Lord is God,
follow him! But if Baal, then follow him. And the people did
not answer him a word.

—1 KINGS 18:21

Like many people, I assumed that doubt and unbelief were the same, because we usually put them in the same context. In recent years, however, I've learned that there is a difference. Obviously, doubt and unbelief do not honor God, but I want to show you how they function in different ways.

The story of the prophet Elijah is an excellent picture of doubt at work. King Ahab was the most evil leader the people had known. Elijah declared that because of Ahab's wickedness, no rain would fall until he, the prophet, said so. For the next three-and-a-half years, drought scourged the land.

Now, that's a pretty clear picture. There had been sufficient rain before Elijah's declaration—but after he spoke, the skies quit yielding water. That is pretty obvious. Who would question God or His prophet? But apparently, the people's fear of

Ahab—as well as the lack of rainfall—caused their minds to be filled with questions.

Elijah finally called all the people together, along with the king and the false prophets, and asked them why they doubted. Why were they caught between two possible answers? That's what doubt really is. Doubt isn't simply unbelief—it's more of an attitude that says, "I believe, but . . ." or, "I want to believe, but . . ."

Doubt often comes to reside where faith once lived. Doubt is active opposition to faith, and it tries to push faith aside. The people had believed the prophet, but as time wore on— three-and-a-half years—apparently questions arose and un-certainty crept in. *If Elijah really did this, he ought to stop it right now. Maybe it just happened.* Or, *How do we really know that was the word of God?* As soon as they seriously asked themselves these questions, they opened the door for Satan to bring doubt into their minds.

Doubt never comes from God—it is always in opposition to His will. In writing to the Romans, Paul pointed out that the Lord gives each of us a measure of faith (see Romans 12:3). When we cling to that faith, we push away doubts. But when we allow questions to enter in—any kind of uncer-tainty that takes our minds away from God's wonderful work in our lives—that's doubt. It is also a subtle, sneaky entry point for our enemy. He plants doubt in our minds, hoping it will cause us to oppose God. We probably don't think of doubt as something that strong, but it is—it's the first step of oppo-sition to what God declares. That's why we need to know

God's Word. If we know the Word, we can recognize it when the devil lies to us and causes us to question.

Elijah wouldn't allow the people of his day to move back and forth from doubt to belief. He made the options clear: Believe the true God or believe a false idol.

Don't fall into the trap of saying you believe in God when your heart is filled with doubts and questions. Choose true faith and say, "Lord, I believe. I may not always understand, but I trust You."

————————

True and faithful God, in the past, I've been weak, allowing Satan to make me question You, Your love, and Your plans for my life. Not only do I ask You to forgive me, but I also ask You to teach me Your Word and strengthen me so that Satan can never trick me again. Thank You for hearing my prayer. Amen.

51

The Sin of Unbelief

[For Abraham, human reason for] hope being gone, hoped in faith that he should become the father of many nations, as he had been promised, So [numberless] shall your descendants be. He did not weaken in faith when he considered the [utter] impotence of his own body, which was as good as dead because he was about a hundred years old, or [when he considered] the barrenness of Sarah's [deadened] womb. No unbelief or distrust made him waver (doubtingly question) concerning the promise of God, but he grew strong and was empowered by faith as he gave praise and glory to God, fully satisfied and assured that God was able and mighty to keep His word and to do what He had promised.

—ROMANS 4:18–21

Doubt, as I've said, raises questions. It makes us ask, "Did God really say . . . ?" "Does the Word really mean . . . ?" Doubt is often the devil's entry point into our minds. Just such simple, easy questions are enough to give Satan a place to attack.

Unbelief is far worse than doubt. Doubt brings in the question, but unbelief is the result. I've watched Satan launch his attacks on Christians by first posing a question and then causing that question to bring doubt. The triumph of sin in the Garden of Eden began just that way. Satan said to Eve, "Can it really be that God has said, You shall not eat from every tree of the garden?" (Genesis 3:1b). That's subtle. Satan doesn't fight with God or argue with the Bible. He just raises a question and allows our minds to do the rest.

When the question comes in such a simple way, the obvious answer *must be,* "Well, He didn't really mean . . ." With that reaction, Satan has established a stronghold in your mind, and it takes little for him to move you from there to a total lack of belief.

I've spoken with people who were led astray in just such a way. They started out as faithful, committed followers of Jesus Christ. But as Satan planted doubt and unbelief in their hearts, they turned their backs on spiritual things. One man said, "I was simple and naïve in those days. I believed anything I heard. I know better now." Satan robbed him of his faith and, in the process, stole his joy and hope.

I am familiar with this battle. Because of my ministry, some people think I have everything all worked out and never have to battle for my faith. I can tell you that no Christian reaches that place this side of heaven. As soon as we let our guard down, even in the slightest, Satan sneaks up behind us and starts whispering his lies to us.

That may be the reason the story of Abraham is such an encouragement to me. When I have my battles with faith and taking God totally at His Word, I often go back and read Romans 4. The example of that godly man is absolutely amazing to me. In the natural, everything appeared to be against God's promises to Abraham. I'm sure Abraham's friends laughed when he said, "God will give me a son." Satan's scoffers must have been in place every day, but Abraham stood the test. The Bible says, "He did not weaken in faith . . . but he grew strong and was empowered by faith as he gave praise and glory to God" (vs. 19-20). I love that statement.

After the Holy Spirit called me into ministry, I was elated—and humbled. I thought, *Who am I that God should call me?* I could think of hundreds of reasons why anyone but Joyce Meyer should be used by God. But I believed in His call, and I had no doubt—not then.

In the months after the call, however, things moved more slowly than I wanted. More times than I can count, I found myself meditating on Abraham and God's promises to him. If a human being like Abraham could believe and not stagger with unbelief, why couldn't Joyce Meyer? I fought the battles, and with God's grace, I won. That's how it is each time—a fresh battle and a new and joyous victory.

God and Father of Abraham, I thank You for Abraham's example. Help me to push aside the devil's advances by totally trusting You and standing on Your promises for my life—even if no one else stands with me. In Jesus' name, I ask. Amen.

52

Defeating Unbelief

Be well balanced (temperate, sober of mind), be vigilant and cautious at all times; for that enemy of yours, the devil, roams around like a lion roaring [in fierce hunger], seeking someone to seize upon and devour. Withstand him; be firm in faith [against his onset—rooted, established, strong, immovable, and determined], knowing that the same (identical) sufferings are appointed to your brotherhood (the whole body of Christians) throughout the world.

—1 PETER 5:8–9

Sometimes we unintentionally give the wrong impression about spiritual warfare. We know that our enemy is the devil and that we must fight daily to win, but that's not everything. If the Christian life were nothing but battles, it would be discouraging to fight every hour of every day.

I would feel that I could never relax because as soon as I did, Satan would sneak back again. That's not the picture I want to present. The Christian life is one of joy and peace. God gives us a great sense of fulfillment, and we're at rest because we know we honor Him by the way we live.

Peter wrote to Christians about their enemy—warning

them and urging them to be vigilant, which is where we often put the emphasis. Just before he wrote those words, however, he said, "Casting the whole of your care [all your anxieties, all your worries, all your concerns, once and for all] on Him, for He cares for you affectionately and cares about you watch-fully" (v. 7). As we read that verse, it tells us that we must re-mind ourselves of God's love for us—God cares. Because God cares, we can trust Him to take care of us.

We need that as part of our foundation. It's not that we don't have faith; it's that Satan tries to destroy our faith with lies like: "If God really cared about you, would He make you go through this trial?" "If God truly loved you, would He treat you this way?"

Those questions that the devil throws at you are full of lies. If he can make you think you're not loved or that God doesn't have your best interests at heart, he can plant tiny seeds of unbelief. God wants you to remain strong and true like Abra-ham and other believers in the Bible.

One of the things I've learned from ministering to thou-sands of people is that the terrible and negative problems striking our lives are not what cause us to turn away from God. No, it's our reaction to those situations that makes the difference. Think of Abraham again. When God promised to give him a son, he was an old man. He could have said, "How could that possibly be? I'm old and long past being able to fa-ther a child." Instead, he said, "That's wonderful! I believe."

When struggles, trials, and hardships come your way—and they always do—you have a choice. You can heed Peter's words and give God your cares, worries, and concerns. No matter how dark the night or how evil the situation, you must remind yourself that God is not only present with you in those situations, but He also loves you and will provide for you.

Your job is to be vigilant during those difficult times. You can rejoice in God's love and blessings when all is going well—and that's what God wants you to do. But in the dark moments, you need to remind yourself that the devil stalks you and wants to defeat you.

One more thing. Sometimes you may wonder why you have so many trials and problems. Is it possible that the devil may have singled you out because of God's great plan for your life? The more faithful you are, the more you have to resist him and his lies of unbelief.

Dear heavenly Father, the enemy often tries to fill me with unbelief and make me deny Your powerful love for me. But like Abraham, I stand firm on Your promises. Thank You for the comfort I find in Your assurance that You're always with me. Amen.

53

Keep Walking on the Water!

*And in the fourth watch [between 3:00—6:00 a.m.] of the
night, Jesus came to them, walking on the sea. And when the
disciples saw Him walking on the sea, they were terrified and
said, It is a ghost! And they screamed out with fright. But
instantly He spoke to them, saying, Take courage! I AM! Stop
being afraid! And Peter answered Him, Lord, if it is You,
command me to come to You on the water.*

—MATTHEW 14:25–28

Let's focus for a moment on this part of a well-known New
Testament story. The disciples were in the middle of the Sea
of Galilee at midnight when they looked up and saw Jesus
walking on the water. That is amazing, but as the story continues, Matthew wrote of the boisterous winds, yet Jesus kept
walking on top of the waves.

The disciples were afraid—and that makes sense. Who
would expect to see anyone walking on top of the water, even
under the best of conditions?

Then Jesus cried out and told them, "Take courage! I AM!
Stop being afraid!" (v. 27). This is the powerful moment in
the story. What will happen now? Do they move over

and give Jesus a place to sit in their boat? Should they get out and join Him on the waves? Do they huddle in fear, reminding themselves that human beings can't walk on top of water?

Peter was the only one who responded in true faith. And let's make no mistake here. For Peter to say, "Lord, if it is You, command me to come to You on the water" (v. 28) was a tremendous act of faith. You'll notice that he was the only one who spoke that way.

That was a powerful moment of faith. It was a defining moment that pointed out Peter's great faith and belief in Jesus, the Anointed One of God. He was so convinced that Jesus truly was the Son of God that he was ready to get out of the boat and walk on top of the water with Him.

How many of you would get out of the boat? I emphasize this because it would be easy enough to *say*, "Lord, I see You walking on the water, and I believe I could walk on the water alongside You." *But would you?* Do you have the kind of faith that would enable you to step out of the boat? Of the twelve disciples, Peter was the only one who took that step of faith.

I'm not citing this example of faith to discourage you or to make you feel that your faith is somehow lacking. I'm simply pointing out the great triumph of a man who dared to believe! Peter believed so strongly that he took a step of faith over the side of the boat and started walking toward Jesus.

Most of us know the rest of the story. Some might even smirk, saying, "Big deal! He got out of the boat, started walking on the water, got scared, and began to sink. And he also received a rebuke from Jesus: 'O you of little faith, why did you doubt?'" (v. 31). But think about it—Jesus didn't say those words to the other disciples. He directed the words "you of little faith" to Peter. The implication is the others had *no* faith at that moment.

Think of these words not just as words of rebuke, but also as words of encouragement to Peter, the one who had enough faith to step out of the boat and begin walking on the water. "But when he perceived and felt the strong wind, he was frightened, and as he began to sink, he cried out, Lord, save me [from death]!" (v. 30).

What if you saw this as Jesus' great encouragement, not just to Peter, but also to you? What if you looked at this event as Jesus saying to you, "You started so well. You believed Me, and got out of the boat. *You did it!* You walked on water just as I did. But then you allowed doubt to enter, and when that happened, you began to sink."

This powerful story is a wonderful reminder that Jesus is always with you, and He will suspend natural laws to reach out to you and care for you.

———

Lord Jesus, please forgive my lack of faith. Increase my faith in Your Word, and help me to trust You enough to follow Your leading. When the circumstances around me threaten to pull me into deep waters of doubt, help me to focus on You. I ask these things in Your holy name. Amen.

54

Time to Worship

He said, Come! So Peter got out of the boat and walked on the water, and he came toward Jesus. But when he perceived and felt the strong wind, he was frightened, and as he began to sink, he cried out, Lord, save me [from death]! Instantly Jesus reached out His hand and caught and held him, saying to him, O you of little faith, why did you doubt? And when they got into the boat, the wind ceased. And those in the boat knelt and worshiped Him, saying, Truly You are the Son of God!

—Matthew 14:29–33

Let's take a closer look at this story. Peter believed and stepped out, and then doubt filled his mind, and he started to sink. His rational mind reminded him that people can't walk on water. As soon as his mind turned from the spiritual and supernatural, he failed.

Jesus had already said, "Take courage . . . Stop being afraid!" (v. 27). Those few words were meant to assure the disciples that both the presence and power of Jesus were there to take care of them. Yet only one man responded—one out of twelve.

Peter stepped out and started walking toward the Master . . .

then he faltered. He focused on the storm instead of the presence of Jesus, who was only a few feet away from him. As soon as he diverted his attention, doubt and unbelief pressed in on him.

I've often wondered if his feet slowly sank into the water or if he instantly plunged downward. The Bible account doesn't give us that information, but it does tell us Jesus' response. He grabbed Peter and saved him from the waves, the wind, and the storm.

Even that's not the end of the story. After Jesus and Peter climbed into the boat, another miracle took place: The storm ceased. It's easy to spiritualize this incident and point out that whenever Jesus is with us, the storms of life cease and peace fills our hearts. That is true, but this was a real storm, not a figurative or spiritual one, and the winds instantly stopped.

Matthew makes a point of telling us what happened *after* the storm. During the storm, Peter exercised faith. He believed and he proved it. The others watched and listened, but there was no response from them.

I believe they were still so scared that they hadn't even moved. They heard Jesus' voice telling them not to be afraid, but still they didn't do anything. No one else moved or spoke a word.

Verse 33 tells us that after the storm, the other disciples knelt and worshiped Jesus. I would certainly hope so! Look at the miracles they witnessed. The storm came, the winds blew, and Jesus came to them, walking on the water. He tried to calm their fears by saying, "Stop being afraid," but they were not ready to hear Him. Only after Peter exhibited his faith and Jesus calmed the storm were they able to say, "Truly You are the Son of God!" I'm glad they were able to say those words—finally. It shows that the message got through. But what took so long? How much proof did they need before they were ready to worship?

How much proof do you need of Jesus' love and presence in your life?

———————————

Lord Jesus, sometimes I'm like one of the fearful disciples, requiring all kinds of proof before I can believe You. How many miracles do I need to see before I can call You the Son of God? Help me to be more like Peter, ready and willing to walk with You in any and all storms of life. Thank You for loving me and encouraging me to follow You in faith. Amen.

55

Why the Storms?

Why are you cast down, O my inner self? And why should you moan over me and be disquieted within me? Hope in God and wait expectantly for Him, for I shall yet praise Him, my Help and my God.

—PSALM 42:5

O God, why do You cast us off forever? Why does Your anger burn and smoke against the sheep of Your pasture?

—PSALM 74:1

As I think about the storms we all face in life, I can understand why people sometimes ask, "Why the storms? Why do we have so many problems and struggles in life? Why do God's people have to deal with so much suffering?"

As I considered these questions, I began to see that Satan plants these questions in our minds. It is his attempt to keep us focused on our problems instead of focusing on the goodness of God. If we persist in asking these questions, we're implying that God may be to blame. I don't think it's wrong to ask God why things happen. The writers of the psalms certainly didn't hesitate to ask.

I think of the story of Jesus when He visited the home of

Mary and Martha after their brother, Lazarus, died. Jesus waited until Lazarus had been dead for four days before He visited. When He arrived, Martha said to Jesus, "Master, if You had been here, my brother would not have died" (John 11:21). She went on to say, "And even now I know that whatever You ask from God, He will grant it to You" (v. 22).

Did she really believe those words? I wonder, because "Jesus said to her, Your brother shall rise again. Martha replied, I know that he will rise again in the resurrection at the last day" (vs. 23-24). She didn't get what Jesus was saying.

I don't want to be unkind to Martha, but she missed it. When Jesus came, she didn't ask, "Why didn't You do something?" Instead she said, "If You had been here—if You had been on the job—he'd be alive."

When Jesus assured her that Lazarus would rise again, she didn't understand that it was going to happen right then. She could focus only on the resurrection. By looking at an event that was still in the future, she missed the real meaning of Jesus' words for the present.

But aren't many of us like Martha? We want our lives to run smoothly, and when they don't, we ask *why?* But we really mean, "God, if You truly loved and cared for me, this wouldn't have happened."

Let's think a little more about the "why" question. For example, when someone dies in an accident, one of the first questions family members ask is why? "Why her? Why now? Why this accident?"

For one moment, let's say God explained the reason.

Would that change anything? Probably not. The loved one is still gone, and the pain is just as severe as it was before. What, then, did you learn from the explanation?

In recent years, I've begun to think that *why* isn't what Christians are really asking God. Is it possible that we're asking, "God, do You love me? Will You take care of me in my sorrow and pain? You won't leave me alone in my pain, will You?" Is it possible that, because we're afraid that God doesn't truly care about us, we ask for explanations?

Instead, we must learn to say, "Lord God, I believe. I don't understand, and I could probably never grasp all the reasons why bad things happen, but I can know for certain that You love me and You are with me—always."

———————

Heavenly Father, instead of asking for answers to the why questions, help me to focus on Your great love for me. When Satan tries to fill my mind with troublesome questions, help me to feel the protection of Your loving, caring arms around me. Help me always to show my gratitude and devotion for all that You do for me. In Jesus' name, I pray. Amen.

56

Doubt Is a Choice

Now the eleven disciples went to Galilee, to the mountain to which Jesus had directed and made appointment with them. And when they saw Him, they fell down and worshiped Him; but some doubted. Jesus approached and, breaking the silence, said to them, All authority (all power of rule) in heaven and on earth has been given to Me. Go then and make disciples of all the nations, baptizing them into the name of the Father and of the Son and of the Holy Spirit, teaching them to observe everything that I have commanded you, and behold, I am with you all the days (perpetually, uniformly, and on every occasion), to the [very] close and consummation of the age. Amen (so let it be).

—Matthew 28:16–20

These verses give us some insights as to what happened immediately after the crucifixion and resurrection of Jesus Christ. We often refer to this passage as the Great Commission. Jesus appeared to His disciples on a particular mountain in Galilee, and He told them that God the Father had given Him all authority in heaven and on earth. He then charged them to go out into the world and make disciples of all nations.

Matthew says that the disciples worshiped Jesus the instant they realized it was actually Him they were seeing. But then he adds the one sad, negative statement in this significant story: *But some doubted.*

How can that be? Judas was dead, but the others—those great Christians who later traveled throughout the known world and taught everyone about Jesus—*doubted?* How could they? Had they not witnessed miracles? Had they not seen the lame walk, the blind eyes opened, the demon-possessed healed? Had they not seen Jesus dying on the cross? Did they not—even now—notice His nail-scarred hands?

The answer to all of these questions, of course, is yes. Yet Matthew still says, "But some doubted." Even these special, anointed, and handpicked followers of Christ struggled with doubt and unbelief.

Is it any wonder then that Jesus referred to the importance of faith on so many occasions? Why would Jesus rebuke these faithful men for not believing? Why would He urge them not to doubt? It was because He knew the hearts of men.

Earlier in his gospel, Matthew described what happened when Jesus saw a fig tree that had leaves but no fruit. A fig tree bears fruit at the same time or before it produces leaves, so it was reasonable for him to expect the tree to be bearing fruit. "And He said to it, Never again shall fruit grow on you! And the fig tree withered up at once" (Matthew 21:19b).

The disciples marveled and asked him, "How is it that the fig tree has withered away all at once?" (v.20).

Jesus' answer about the fig tree also applies to faith. "Truly

I say to you, if you have faith (a firm relying trust) and do not doubt, you will not only do what has been done to the fig tree, but even if you say to this mountain, Be taken up and cast into the sea, it will be done" (v. 21).

His point is this: When we believe and do not doubt, we can accomplish miracles. Abraham believed, and God honored his faithfulness. Faith is a gift of God, but doubt is a choice. Doubt is a result of thoughts formed in the mind that are in direct opposition to God's Word. That is why it is so important for us to know the Word of God. We are immediately able to discern the devil's lies when we know the Word. Doubt is just another part of the devil's arsenal of weapons aimed against our minds.

Throughout this book, I've pointed out that we can choose our thoughts. We have the option to decide whether to accept or reject our thoughts. That means when doubt knocks on the door of our minds, we have the option of inviting it in or calmly but firmly dismissing it. The choice is ours. We can believe or we can doubt. And we know the path of believing leads to the blessings of God.

Dear Lord Jesus, I have allowed doubt to enter my mind; many times I have allowed Satan to torture me through my thoughts. I confess these things and ask for Your forgiveness. Now I ask You to fill me with faith and enable me to push away such thoughts. I rejoice that I believe only in You. Amen.

57

A Tempting Offer

Then Jesus was led (guided) by the [Holy] Spirit into the
wilderness (desert) to be tempted (tested and tried) by the
devil. And He went without food for forty days and forty
nights, and later He was hungry.

—MATTHEW 4:1–2

After Jesus had gone through a forty-day fast, Satan approached Him with three tempting offers. The devil came to Jesus when he was weak and hungry. It's natural to assume that the Lord was physically weakened after being without nourishment for such an extended period of time, so, of course, the devil's first offer involved food. "If You are God's Son, command these stones to be made [loaves of] bread" (v. 3).

Later Jesus performed several miracles that included food, such as changing a boy's lunch into enough fish and bread to feed five thousand people and, at another time, to feed four thousand. All of Jesus' miracles were for the good of others. He never performed miracles for Himself or to satisfy any need of His own. That's one major lesson we learn from His temptation.

The devil then took Jesus to a mountaintop and showed

Him the nations of the earth. He said, in effect, "You can have it all in exchange for one slight, easily excusable act. Worship me—just once—and You can have it all." I can even imagine the devil saying, "It's all right; God will understand. You're so weak right now."

It was as if Satan said, "You're going to rule it all anyway. This is just a shortcut." He implied that through one simple act of worship, Jesus could avoid the rejection, the suffering, and even the horrifying death on the cross. And either way, He would achieve the same goal.

As attractive as the offer may have sounded, Jesus turned it down. He recognized the deliberately crafted lie, and Jesus never hesitated. The world would be won for God, but it would be won by the way of sacrifice and obedience. The way of the cross would be Jesus' pathway to victory.

Again, Jesus teaches us that His is not the easy way. Instead, we must take the right way. Whenever the devil tries to convince us there is an easier way—one that will make life better for us—we know we don't want to listen.

As we read the story, the choice seems obvious. But suppose you had been in that wilderness for forty days and nights without food and water. Suppose you had faced such great temptations. Suppose the devil had whispered in your ear, "Just this one time and no one will know."

This is one of the enemy's most subtle lies. Not only does he tempt you to give in and to receive the things you'd like to have, but he also makes it sound simple and easy: "Just do this one thing, and it's all yours."

God never works that way. He wants you to have the best and only the best, but it has to come in the right way.

At the end of the temptation accounts, Matthew inserts a powerful statement. With each temptation, Jesus won because he relied on the Word of God for His strength. And the devil couldn't fight the Word. Finally, Matthew records, "Then the devil departed from Him, and behold, angels came and ministered to Him" (v. 11).

The wisdom to be gleaned from this experience is powerful. Even after you've been battered and tempted, God doesn't leave you. He remains with you to comfort you, to minister to your needs, and to encourage you. Never forget that He is as close to you as the mention of His name. He will never leave you nor forsake you.

Blessed Lord Jesus, thank You for winning the victory over the devil. Thank You for not listening to Satan and for standing on the Word of God in the midst of every temptation. Lord, in Your name, I pray for the wisdom and the strength to defeat the same enemy when he tempts me. Amen

58

The Disobedience of Unbelief

*And Elisha said to him, Take bow and arrows. And he took
bow and arrows. And he said to the king of Israel, Put your
hand upon the bow. And he put his hand upon it, and Elisha
put his hands upon the king's hands. And he said, Open the
window to the east. And he opened it. Then Elisha said,
Shoot. And he shot. And he said, The Lord's arrow of victory,
the arrow of victory over Syria. For you shall smite the
Syrians in Aphek till you have destroyed them. Then he
said, Take the arrows. And he took them. And he said to
the king of Israel, Strike on the ground. And he struck
three times and stopped. And the man of God was angry
with him and said, You should have struck five or six times;
then you would have struck down Syria until you had
destroyed it. But now you shall strike Syria down only
three times.*

—2 Kings 13:15–19

It's easy to say, "I believe," but the true test comes when we
have to act on what we believe. In this story, the king came to
Elisha the prophet to seek his help in obtaining deliverance
from the Syrians. The prophet told him to strike arrows on
the ground as a symbol of Israel's attacks against their enemy,

but the king stopped after shooting only three arrows onto the ground.

Unbelief is disobedience. Period. Had the king believed, he would have struck arrows on the ground many times. Because of his unbelief, he stopped before he'd even gotten a good start. It is not surprising that Elisha became frustrated and angry with him.

Incidents of unbelief are recorded throughout the Old and New Testaments. Unbelief seems to be at work in nearly every direction we turn. Matthew 17:14-20 records the story of a man who brought his epileptic son to Jesus for healing. He said, "And I brought him to Your disciples, and they were not able to cure him" (v. 16).

This boy's father was hurt and disappointed in the disciples' lack of ability to emulate their Leader. We might have agreed with him had we been in his place that day. After all, Jesus had been traveling with these twelve men for several months. They had repeatedly observed as He performed miracles wherever they went. In Luke 10, we learn that Jesus sent out other followers, and they performed a number of miracles and healings. Why couldn't the disciples do them in this instance? Jesus had constantly encouraged them to heal the sick and do the things that He did.

Yet they were unable to heal the boy, and Jesus said: "O you unbelieving (warped, wayward, rebellious) and thoroughly perverse generation! How long am I to remain with you? How long am I to bear with you? Bring him here to Me" (v. 17).

Jesus cast out the demon, and the boy was cured. Unbelief leads to disobedience.

But here's the end of the story. When the disciples asked Jesus why they couldn't heal the boy, Jesus' answer was clear: "Because of the littleness of your faith [that is, your lack of firmly relying trust] . . ." (v. 20).

I feel sure that Jesus' answer caused the disciples to examine their hearts and to ask what held them back. Why didn't they believe? Perhaps they had allowed negative thinking to enter their minds. Perhaps they weren't able to grasp the fact that Jesus wanted to use them and empower them to perform miracles.

Of course, we know from reading the book of Acts that once they were filled with the Holy Spirit, the disciples demonstrated God's supernatural power at work—but not in this story. He said to them, "I assure you, most solemnly I tell you, if anyone steadfastly believes in Me, he will himself be able to do the things that I do; and he will do even greater things than these, because I go to the Father" (John 14:12).

The promise remains valid to this day. Unbelief will keep us from doing what God has called and anointed us to accomplish in life. It will also hinder us from experiencing the sense of peace He wants us to enjoy as we find rest for our souls in Him (see Matthew 11:28,29 KJV).

When God tells us we can do something, we must believe that we can. It is not by our power or our might that we are able to do what He tells us to, but by His Spirit working on the inside of us that we win in the battle of unbelief.

———————————

Lord Jesus, forgive my lack of faith. I know that when I don't believe, I am disobeying You. In Your name, I ask You to help me push away every bit of unbelief so that I may focus on faithfully following You. Amen.

59

A Sabbath Rest

For he who has once entered [God's] rest also has ceased from [the weariness and pain] of human labors, just as God rested from those labors peculiarly His own. Let us therefore be zealous and exert ourselves and strive diligently to enter that rest [of God, to know and experience it for ourselves], that no one may fall or perish by the same kind of unbelief and disobedience [into which those in the wilderness fell].

—HEBREWS 4:10–11

Under the Old Covenant, the Lord required the people of Israel to observe the Sabbath every week. They were to do no work from sundown Friday until sundown Saturday. It was a symbol to them of rest. Throughout the Old Testament, God says that He created the world in six days and ceased from His labors on the seventh.

The writer of the book of Hebrews used the idea of Sabbath as a way of talking about a rest that is available to God's people. In chapter 3, he wrote about Israel's unbelief and quoted from Psalm 95:11: "Accordingly, I swore in My wrath and indignation, They shall not enter into My rest.

[Therefore beware] brethren, take care, lest there be in any one of you a wicked, unbelieving heart [which refuses to cleave to, trust in, and rely on Him], leading you to turn away and desert or stand aloof from the living God" (Hebrews 3:11–12).

The book of Hebrews makes it clear that although the Israel of old saw God at work every day in their lives and enjoyed the divine provision of manna and water and every other need they had, they still did not believe. The Israelites could not enter into that rest—that Sabbath.

Hebrews four makes it clear that the Sabbath rest—the peace of God—is still available to all believers. It is the privilege of every believer to refuse to worry or have anxiety. As believers, we can enter the rest of God. The promise is unchanged. The danger is that we may fail to reach it because of disobedience and unbelief.

The writer uses the word *rest* to mean more than just not working. It also implies setting aside those things that trouble our minds. In other words, to enter the Sabbath rest, we must not allow anything to prevent us from fully enjoying God's peace.

Isn't it interesting that although the Israelites regularly read the Ten Commandments and felt that they followed the Law, either they didn't get what God was saying or—more likely—they didn't believe it. God commanded them not to work, but it wasn't just that He wanted them to take some time off. He was instructing them to do something far more important—to cease the daily routine of their busy lives and spend the Sabbath resting and reflecting on His abundant provision.

I know some people—and I'm sure you do, as well—who work every day of the year. They seem almost afraid to let up, as if they might lose momentum or money or not have enough to provide for their needs. Some people take on two or three side jobs for extra income, even though they don't really need the money. It's as though they think some measure of peace and happiness will come if they have accumulated enough "things" in life.

Sooner or later, they will find that peace doesn't come that way. The Sabbath rest is God's way of saying, "I'm in charge. I'll take care of you if you'll trust Me."

And how do we trust God? One way is to begin to understand the importance of setting aside time to let our minds get quiet enough to recognize that God is truly with us. We don't need to worry or be anxious about paying our bills or having enough food to eat. As long as we worry and fret about those things, we aren't living in the Sabbath rest of God.

I am not suggesting that people quit their jobs and just sit around reflecting on the goodness of God. I believe we are to work hard and do our best at whatever God has given us to do. But ultimately, it is God's love, His peace, and His provision that will see us through. The devil will whisper that it depends on us and we have to do it all. But once we have entered into the Sabbath rest, we *know* that God is the One who provides, and we can truly rest and enjoy our lives.

O Holy One of Israel, forgive me. Too often, I worry or fret about not having enough. You are my God. You will always assure me that my needs are taken care of. My concern is to enter into Your Sabbath rest and take pleasure in Your presence. In the name of Jesus Christ, enable me to live in that Sabbath rest. Amen.

60

From Faith to Faith

*For I am not ashamed of the Gospel (good news) of Christ,
for it is God's power working unto salvation [for deliverance
from eternal death] to everyone who believes with a personal
trust and a confident surrender and firm reliance. . . . For in
the Gospel, a righteousness that God ascribes is revealed,
both springing from faith and leading to faith [disclosed
through the way of faith that arouses to more faith]. As it is
written, The man who through faith is just and upright shall
live and shall live by faith.*

—ROMANS 1:16–17

Faith is a word the apostle Paul used often in his writing.
When writing to the Thessalonians, he wanted to know
about their faith. While the word *faith* means belief or absolute trust, it's more than that—the word also implies loy-
alty and commitment.

Faith means being convinced that something is true. In 1
Corinthians 15:17, the apostle told the Corinthians that if
Jesus did not rise from the dead, their faith was meaningless.
He was saying that all they believed was utterly useless. True
faith acknowledges that the message of Jesus' death and res-
urrection is true.

True faith begins when we're receptive—when we're willing to listen. It starts with a kind of mental assent—it seems reasonable that it's true. But that's not true faith. True faith happens when we say, "Not only does it make sense to me, but I'm willing to stake my life on it."

Paul quoted from Habakkuk 2:4, saying that the just—the righteous—shall live by faith. One way to think of the just is to think of those who were "justified," or made right, by the death of Jesus Christ on the cross. If we are justified, it means that God treats us as though we are not and have never been sinners. He treats us as His own—His beloved children. Instead of being God's enemies, we're His friends. Instead of fighting Him, we serve Him.

When God calls us just, or righteous, we enter into a relationship of love, confidence, and friendship. We need not fear or worry because there is no punishment for us.

When Paul says the one "who through faith is just and upright shall live and shall live by faith," he means that those of us who have been made right with God live by our faith. That is, we live by our trust in the God who reaches out to us.

This is where many must fight the wiles of Satan. Instead of focusing on all God has done for us, they listen to the devil whisper, "Do you remember when you lost your temper?" "You're worried about paying your bills, and if you worry, you don't have faith, right?" "If you're supposed to be a Christian, how could you have said what you did?"

The torments are there, and the devil never passes up the opportunity to remind us of past failures. All have failed, and we will continue to fail, but when we do, we can repent and move on.

I went through a particularly difficult time several years ago when there was absolutely no joy or peace in my life. Unhappiness filled most of my days. I repeatedly asked the Lord what was wrong with me, really wanting to know what my problem was . . . no kidding around. I was working so hard to please the Lord and trying to be the kind of Christian I thought I should be, but I certainly didn't feel like any progress was being made.

Then one day, I came across Romans 15:13 in a box of scripture cards: "May the God of your hope so fill you with all joy and peace in believing [through the experience of your faith] that by the power of the Holy Spirit you may abound and be overflowing (bubbling over) with hope." That was it! I got it!

I had plunged into doubt and unbelief, allowing the devil to torment me with his evil lies. As a result, I had become negative, grouchy, short-tempered, and impatient. I was making myself miserable, and the devil was thrilled at the stronghold he had over me!

This scripture changed all of that old thinking! I knew the answer. Jesus loved me so much that He not only forgave all my sins of the past, but He also looked ahead and forgave me for those moments of weakness when I'd fail in the future. I'm not referring to deliberate sin, but to human weaknesses, those times when I just don't live up to all the truth I know.

"Just think," I told my husband, "two thousand years

ago Jesus not only died on the cross for all my sins before I even knew Him, but for all of my sins and failures until the day I meet Him face to face." That was such a powerful thought to me.

Then I pondered the words of Paul quoted at the beginning of this meditation: "For in the gospel, a righteousness which God ascribes is revealed, both springing from faith and leading to faith [disclosed through the way of faith that arouses to more faith]." I finally understood the concept of living from faith to faith. I don't have to allow Satan to sneak in with questions or unbelief. I can live every moment moving from faith to more faith to more faith.

———————————

Lord Jesus Christ, I am in awe of Your love for me,
which is so great and so powerful that You not only died
for all my sins before I was born, but You've provided
for all my weak moments in the future. I am so thankful
to You for Your love, and I rejoice in Your holy name.
Amen.

61

Don't Let the Devil Steal It

For it is like a man who was about to take a long journey, and
he called his servants together and entrusted them with his
property. . . . He who had received one talent also came
forward, saying, Master, I knew you to be a harsh and hard
man, reaping where you did not sow, and gathering where you
had not winnowed [the grain]. So I was afraid, and I went and
hid your talent in the ground. Here you have what is your own.

—MATTHEW 25:14; 24–25

Jesus often gave people illustrations containing life lessons
that could be applied to common situations in which most
anyone can find themselves at any given time. The Parable of
the Talents is such an illustration. A *talent* was the type of
currency used in Jesus' day. One talent is said to have been
worth more than a thousand dollars. This particular parable
describes a man who gave certain amounts of money to three
of his servants with the instruction to invest it.

I find two very interesting points in this story. First, the
landowner distributed the money according to each person's
ability. He didn't try to burden his workers with more than they
were capable of handling. The two men to whom he gave the
most money invested wisely and doubled their investments.

Upon the landowner's return, they were made full partners in the business. The second thing I realized is that the two with the most ability used it wisely and were richly rewarded. The third man—the one with the least ability—failed.

Think about this. God didn't ask the third man to invest five talents or even three. He knew this man wasn't capable of handling such a task. He gave the third servant the least amount of responsibility, and that man still failed. Worse, he tried to justify his failure by blaming the master! But he also said something else—and that's the secret to understanding this story: "I was afraid and hid your talent in the ground" (see v. 25).

He didn't lose the money, but he did nothing with it. And the master responded, "You wicked and lazy and idle servant!" (v. 26). The spirit of fear had caused the man to do nothing.

Let's turn that around. The owner said, "Then you should have invested my money with the bankers, and at my coming I would have received what was my own with interest" (v. 27). Suppose the man had gone to the bank and invested as the owner suggested. He would never have made as much profit as the other two. And that would have been all right, because all that the owner asked was for him to do what he could— what was reasonably expected of him.

That's one way the devil snares us. He causes us to compare ourselves with others and see how much money or talents they have. Or he tells us other people are given more opportunities than we will ever have. But God doesn't ask us to do what someone else does. He asks us to use the gifts and abilities that He has given to us.

I truly believe that God has a plan for each of our lives. A life lived in faith and obedience to God's Word causes His plan to unfold before our eyes. Clutching what little we have in fear won't allow us to fulfill God's plan. In fact, this kind of mindset allows the devil to lie to us and cause us to give up on our dreams and God's plan for our lives.

Fear only supplies the characteristics of the idle, lazy, and wicked servant. When we listen to the devil, we soon believe we can do nothing. He'll convince us that everything we attempt will fail. If we listen to God, we will hear the words of the Lord: "Well done, you upright (honorable, admirable) and faithful servant! You have been faithful and trustworthy over a little; I will put you in charge of much. Enter into and share the joy (the delight, the blessedness) which your master enjoys" (v. 21). It is not how much we accomplish that is important, but it's being faithful to the ability God has given us that makes the difference.

Loving and caring Father, I don't know which of those three men I'm the most like in terms of my ability. But I pray that You will make me faithful to fulfill Your plan for my life. In the name of Your Son, Jesus, I thank You for helping me. Thank You, Lord, for helping me keep the enemy from stealing the little or the much You have given me. Amen.

62

Anxious Minds

Therefore do not worry and be anxious, saying, What are we going to have to eat? or, What are we going to have to drink? or, What are we going to have to wear? For the Gentiles (heathen) wish for and crave and diligently seek all these things, and your heavenly Father knows well that you need them all. But seek (aim at and strive after) first of all His kingdom and His righteousness (His way of doing and being right), and then all these things taken together will be given you besides.

—Matthew 6:31–33

The word *worry* is defined as a feeling of uneasiness or a troubled, anxious, distressed, and concerned mind. Another definition I have heard for *worry* is "to torment oneself with disturbing thoughts." When I heard the last definition, I immediately decided that I am smart enough to know better than to sit around tormenting myself! I believe the enemy uses worry and anxiety to distract us from the call of God on our lives.

Sadly, far too many people may actually be addicted to worrying. I have a friend who worries beyond all reason. He admits that his mother *taught* him to worry. He doesn't remember a time in his entire life when his mother wasn't worried about something that had happened, was happening, or was about to happen. I have to admit that I was once just like this. If I didn't have something to worry about, I worried about someone else's problems.

I didn't know what it meant to live in peace. I am convinced that it is absolutely impossible to worry and to live in peace at the same time. Yet I often see people trying to do both.

They've gotten so used to worrying that they apply this condition to almost every function of their lives. For some people, it can be something as simple as fretting over getting to a meeting on time. For others, it can mean being nervous about meeting someone for the first time or the discomfort of going for a job interview. I hear the word *worry* used all the time.

What if we were to use the word *torment*? If we think of worry as satanic torment or mental torture, we get closer to the biblical idea. Think of agony and suffering as part of torment. Isn't that exactly how Satan works? Of course, he works at not letting us identify him as the source. It's easier for him to torment us if we blame our neighbors, children, parents, or coworkers. "If they would just leave me alone and give me peace," we say. As long as we see the agitation coming from someone else or a situation we can't do anything about, we live in torment. That's when the devil preys on us and makes it even worse.

The apostle John wrote about love, saying that if we truly love one another, God abides in us, and His love has been perfected in us. But notice this: "And we know (understand, recognize, are conscious of, by observation and by experience) and believe (adhere to and put faith in and rely on) the love God cherishes for us. God is love, and he who dwells and continues in love dwells and continues in God, and God dwells and continues in him. . . . There is no fear in love [dread does not exist], but full-grown (complete, perfect) love turns fear out of doors and expels every trace of terror! For fear brings with it the thought of punishment, and [so] he who is afraid has not reached the full maturity of love [is not yet grown into love's complete perfection]" (1 John 4:16, 18).

These are all strong words, and I'm quoting them for a reason. If the devil can convince you that worry is a small thing, you don't take it too seriously. "Oh, everybody worries a little," you say, brushing it off.

No, not everyone worries. Worry is a tool of the devil, so it's not something that you, as a Christian, need to tolerate. Worry is nothing but a satanic attack on your mind. It does not accomplish any good thing.

More often than not, there is nothing you can do about the things that concern you. They're beyond your control. You can worry about your future or your children's marriages or whether your company will close and lay you off. But there's nothing you can do in the natural about these things. It is a far better plan to spend the time and energy you would spend worrying on reminding yourself of God's promise: "You will guard him and keep him in perfect and constant peace whose mind . . . is stayed on You, because he commits himself to You" (Isaiah 26:3).

A faith-filled missionary family in Africa dealt with the issue of worry in a very creative way. Whenever anyone started to worry about anything, the parents and their three children would go to the front door and each of them would make a strong kicking movement and say aloud, "Devil, get out of our house. We belong to God, and we don't have to let you come inside." I like that. Use the authority over the enemy that God gave you. Start today!

Holy God, please forgive me for allowing the devil to torment me in any way—and especially for tolerating his tricks in small worries and anxieties. In the name of Jesus, I ask You to enable me to kick him and his tricks out of my life. Amen.

63

Greater Things

Therefore I tell you, stop being perpetually uneasy (anxious and worried) about your life, what you shall eat or what you shall drink; or about your body, what you shall put on. Is not life greater [in quality] than food, and the body [far above and more excellent] than clothing? . . . And who of you by worrying and being anxious can add one unit of measure (cubit) to his stature or to the span of his life?

—MATTHEW 6:25, 27

The devil is constantly waging war on the battlefield of the mind. Our soul is the tangible area between our spirit—the place where God Himself lives—and our physical body. It is made up of our mind, will, and emotions—it tells us what we think, what we want, and how we feel. When our mind is constantly stirred up with concern, worry, and anxiety, our God-given inner voice of insight and understanding becomes drowned out. In this unstable state, we no longer know what God's will is regarding what we should and shouldn't do.

When we allow the devil to overtake our mind with worry and anxiety instead of following God's Spirit, we are living the life of the flesh, and it keeps us out of God's will.

Romans 8:8 says that ". . . those who are living the life of the flesh [catering to the appetites and impulses of their carnal nature] cannot please or satisfy God, or be acceptable to Him." This does not mean that God doesn't love us. It simply means that He is not satisfied with, nor will He accept, fleshly behavior.

God cares about us and about our needs. He wants greater things for us than we want for ourselves. We must fight hard to resist the temptation to accept the devil's endless lies. When I finally got fed up with not having any peace in my life, I made a decision to do whatever I needed to do to get it. I asked God what I should do. His response was clear: "Joyce, you need to begin living on a deeper level." Eventually, the Lord made it apparent to me that the deeper level on which I needed to live was the level of the Spirit.

In order for us to truly enjoy the abundant life Jesus died to give us, we need to stop worrying about what we think we want and need, and start following the promptings of the Holy Spirit. That's the message against worry. It doesn't matter if your need is food, a job, the right clothing, the best schools for your children, your future, or the future of your family—God knows and God cares. The trick of Satan is to whisper, "God doesn't care about you. If God truly cared, you wouldn't be in this mess."

When we focus on ourselves—*what we don't have*—we have little energy left to focus on others and reaching out to help them. We don't give money freely when we're afraid or worried that we'll lose our job or not have enough to pay our own bills. But when we trust God to provide for every need, we are free to share what we have.

Let me encourage you to stop worrying about your own needs and instead focus on the Word of God. You might even need to say to yourself out loud, "God does love me, and nothing can separate me from His love. He has heard my confession of sin, and He has forgiven and cleansed me. God has a positive plan for my future because His Word says so" (see Romans 8:38-39; 1 John 1:9; Jeremiah 29:11).

Every time worry and anxiety come up to try and steal your righteousness, peace, and joy, find out what the Word of God says, and then open your mouth and speak the Word. God's ultimate goal is to get us to the point where no matter what is going on, we remain calm. Who is going to keep us calm? The answer to that question is the power of the Holy Spirit working on the inside of us. God wants us to develop the habit of running to Him for the grace to resist the lies of the devil. Eventually the truth will win out and change our life!

———————————

My heavenly Father, thank You for caring for me and for assuring me that You will provide for every need I have. Too often, I've allowed worry to creep in and steal my joy or my peace. Because of worries over little things, sometimes I've been unable to focus on the greater things in this life You do for me. In the name of Jesus Christ, free me from the things that bind me so I can be totally free to worship and serve You. Amen.

64

Reminders

That is why I would remind you to stir up (rekindle the embers of, fan the flame of, and keep burning) the [gracious] gift of God, [the inner fire] that is in you. . . . For God did not give us a spirit of timidity (of cowardice, of craven and cringing and fawning fear), but [He has given us a spirit] of power and of love and of calm and well-balanced mind and discipline and self-control.

—2 TIMOTHY 1:6–7

It doesn't matter what kind of problem we have in our lives, we need self-control and discipline to gain and maintain the victory. I believe this is especially true with regard to our thought life and the battle for our mind. What begins in the mind eventually comes out of the mouth, and before we know it, we're telling anyone who will listen how we feel. We have to discipline our mind, our mouth, our feelings, and our actions so that they are all in agreement with what the Word of God says.

Every quality of God that is in you and me, God Himself planted in us in the form of a seed the day we accepted Christ (see Colossians 2:10). Over time and through life's experiences, the seeds of Christ's character begin to grow and produce the fruit of His Spirit: love, joy, peace, patience, kindness, goodness, faithfulness, gentleness, and self-control (see Galatians 5:22–23).

I have found that it is virtually impossible to operate in any of the other eight fruit of the Spirit unless we are exercising self-control. How can you and I remain *patient,* for example, in the midst of an upsetting situation unless we exercise restraint? Or how can we walk in *love* and believe the best of someone after they have repeatedly hurt us unless we use the fruit of self-control?

As Christians, we have the fruit of the Spirit in us, but we must purposely choose to exercise them. Not choosing to exercise the fruit of the Spirit is what produces carnal Christians—those who are under the control of ordinary impulses and walk after the desires of the flesh (see 1 Corinthians 3:3). Whatever we exercise the most becomes the strongest.

Our thoughts and words are two areas in which the Holy Spirit is constantly prompting us to exercise self-control. The Bible says that ". . . as [a man] thinks in his heart, so is he," and "out of the abundance (overflow) of the heart his mouth speaks" (Proverbs 23:7; Luke 6:45b). The devil is constantly trying to get us to accept wrong thoughts about everything from God's love for us (or the lack of it) to what terrible thing is going to happen to us next. Why? Because he knows that once we start accepting and believing his lies, it is just a matter of time until we begin to speak them out of our mouths. And when we speak wrong things, we open the door for wrong things to come into our lives (see Proverbs 18:20–21).

What if, instead of allowing our minds to go over all of the things that have hurt us, we would remind ourselves to think about all the good things God has brought into our lives? When we allow Satan to fill our minds with worry, anxiety, and doubt, we wear out our ability to make good decisions. Worry is also thankless by nature. I've noticed that people who worry rarely see much good in life. They talk about tragedy, failures, sickness, and loss. They seem unable to focus on the good things that they still have in life.

Try this. Each day, focus on the things God has done for you in the past. This will make it easier for you to expect good things in the future. As I wrote those words, I thought of the memorials mentioned in the Old Testament. Often the people stacked up heaps of stones as reminders that God had delivered them or appeared to them. As they looked backward and remembered, they were able to look forward and believe.

The psalmist wrote, "O my God, my life is cast down upon me [and I find the burden more than I can bear]; therefore will I [earnestly] remember You from the land of the Jordan [River] and the [summits of Mount] Hermon" (Psalm 42:6). He was reminding himself of past victories. When he was having problems, he recalled God's great work in the lives of the people.

When doubts try to sneak in, you can do what the psalmist did: You can look back and remember that God has always been with His people. All of us have had times when we wondered if we'd make it. But we did. So will you.

———————

My great God, forgive me for allowing the little things of life to distract me and to take my thoughts away from You. Through Jesus Christ, help me always to remember that You are with me in the good times and in the bad times. Amen.

65

Our Responsibility—God's Responsibility

So do not worry or be anxious about tomorrow, for tomorrow will have worries and anxieties of its own. Sufficient for each day is its own trouble.

—Matthew 6:34

Every believer has the responsibility to live right—to be a doer of the Word and not just a hearer. Motivated by the reverential fear of the Lord, we can learn to live carefully and begin to make a difference in the world we live in. You and I need to be careful about what we allow into our spirits and how we live our lives. Proverbs 4:23 says to guard our heart with all diligence because out of it flows the issues of life. I believe we should have a careful attitude about how we live— not a casual or a careless one. We need to be careful about what we watch, what we listen to, what we think about, and who our friends are.

I'm not saying we need to live according to the strict and demanding dictates of man. Some would say we must not wear makeup or that we must wear colorless clothing from our necks to our ankles. That is nothing more than legalistic bondage to a bunch of rules and regulations. I had a very legalistic relationship with God for years and was miserable, so the last thing I want to do is teach legalism. What I am saying is that we shouldn't compromise. We should recognize our responsibility as Christians to live our lives in such a way that unbelievers will be attracted to God by our behavior.

James 4:17 says, ". . . any person who knows what is right to do but does not do it, to him it is sin." In other words, if we are convicted that something is wrong, then we must not do it—even if we see a hundred other people doing it and getting by with it. They may *seem* to be getting by with it, but sooner or later, we will all reap what we sow.

We know that worry and anxiety are not characteristics of a godly Christian. Yet still, many Christians worry. You can choose to worry, or you can reject worry and choose to live with joy and peace. Most people don't want to hear that message, and they seem to find an odd comfort in thinking that worrying is beyond their control. It is not. *Worry is a sin against God.*

As long as I've been in the church, I don't think I've ever heard anyone make that statement. But it is sin. It is calling God a liar. It is saying that God is not sufficiently able to take care of you and provide for your needs.

Faith says, "God can do it." Worry says, "God isn't able to help me."

When you worry, you not only call God a liar, but you have also allowed the devil to fill your mind with anxious thoughts. The more you focus on the problems, the larger they become. You start to fret and may even end up in despair.

Think of the words of the great apostle: "I have strength for all things in Christ Who empowers me [I am ready for anything and equal to anything through Him Who infuses inner strength into me; I am self-sufficient in Christ's sufficiency]" (Philippians 4:13). Or think of the words from the psalmist: "Commit your way to the Lord [roll and repose each care of your load on Him]; trust (lean on, rely on, and be confident) also in Him and He will bring it to pass" (Psalm 37:5).

Jesus told His disciples not to be anxious and, as quoted above, not to worry about tomorrow. But He did more than teach those words; He lived them out: "And Jesus replied to him, Foxes have holes and the birds of the air have lodging places, but the Son of Man has nowhere to lay His head" (Matthew 8:20). That wasn't a complaint but a simple fact of life. Jesus trusted His Father's provision for Him even when He didn't know where He would sleep or what He would eat.

Jesus taught that we are not to worry about anything in life. He wasn't speaking about planning and thinking ahead. He was saying that some people never act because fear holds them back. They can always tell you ten things that can go wrong with every plan. Jesus wants us to live a stress-free life. If you are worrying about what might happen, you're hindering God from working in your life.

I heard about a couple whose daughter was diagnosed with a serious illness that wasn't covered by insurance. The parents were struggling to pay all the medical bills. Not knowing what else to do, they both went into their bedroom for a lengthy time of prayer. Afterward the husband said, "It was really quite simple. I am God's servant. My responsibility is to serve my Master. His responsibility is to take care of me."

The next day, the doctors told them that their daughter was eligible to be part of an experimental surgery and all expenses would be paid. The wife smiled and said, "God is responsible, isn't He?" What a testimony to their faith and trust in God who remains faithful and responsible at all times and in all things. God is no respecter of persons. What He does for one, He will do for another (see Romans 2:11). I encourage you to stop worrying and start trusting in Him.

Lord God, I know that worry is a sin against You. In the name of Jesus, help me overcome all anxieties and worry and enable me to trust You to provide for every need I have. Amen.

66

Right from the Heart

Therefore do not worry and be anxious, saying, What are we going to have to eat? or, What are we going to have to drink? or, What are we going to have to wear?

—MATTHEW 6:31

"What are you going to do?" As a Christian leader, I've come to believe this is one of Satan's favorite questions. I sometimes think he sends out special demons that have one specific task: to whisper this question in the ears of believers: "What are you going to do?" If you listen, the questions increase. The more they increase, the more negative and intense they become. Before long, you think of every possible obstacle on your path. You begin to feel as if nothing is right in your life.

That is the devil's task. He and his helpers wage war on the battlefield of your mind. They want to engage you and other Christians in long, drawn-out, costly combat. The more questions and uncertainties they raise, the greater their chances for victory over your mind.

Jesus instructs us to ". . . stop being perpetually uneasy (anxious and worried) about your life, what you shall eat or what you shall drink; or about your body, what you shall put on. Is not life greater [in quality] than food, and the body [far above and more excellent] than clothing?" (v. 25).

The first thing you need to remind yourself of is that you are living in disobedience when you allow anxieties to fill your mind. Jesus says, "Don't do that."

Second, remind yourself that when you worry, you're looking at the wrong things. In school, most of us were shown pictures that were optical illusions. If we looked at a picture one way, we saw a woman's face. If we looked at it differently, we saw a rose.

Think of that as a mindset. If you focus on Jesus and His loving arms stretched out to you, you live in peace. You know He's with you, and if He's with you, He will also take care of you. If you focus on the other picture, you see only problems, defeats, and discouragement. It really does depend on where you concentrate your attention.

The enemy knows that if he can feed your mind often enough and long enough with the wrong things, he can make you think about and feel only the wrong things. For instance, instead of being thankful that the Lord has been with you through many dark and troublesome times, you can begin to ask, "How did I get here anyway? What am I doing in this fix? If God really loved me. . . ."

That's not the end of it. Once the devil starts to win in the area of poisoning your mind, he moves on, and before long, you're repeating Satan's words—words that not only tear you down, but also hurt and tear down others. Then Satan has a double victory—he's trapped you, and you've influenced others.

Jesus said to the people of His day, "You offspring of vipers! How can you speak good things when you are evil (wicked)? For out of the fullness (the overflow, the superabundance) of the heart the mouth speaks. The good man from his inner good treasure flings forth good things, and the evil man out of his inner evil storehouse flings forth evil things" (Matthew 12:34–35).

Those are strong, powerful words. They remind us that the devil starts with a whisper—just the smallest word of doubt in your ear. If you listen, his words get louder and you hear more things. Soon you unconsciously listen for his misdirection.

That leads you to speak the words in your heart, whatever they are. Once you speak, you move into action. You not only spoil your own relationship with God, but you become instruments to churn up doubts and fears in others.

There is only one way for you to win: Refuse to listen to Satan. As soon as you hear such words, you need to say, "Satan, the Lord rebuke you. Stay out of my mind."

———————

Lord Jesus, thank You for Your words that remind me of the importance of my thoughts and my words. Please, I ask in Your name, fill my heart with such an abundance of peace and joy that the enemy can never infiltrate my mind. May my words reflect Your presence in my life. Amen.

67

Seek God, Not Gifts

In Gibeon the Lord appeared to Solomon in a dream by night.
And God said, Ask what I shall give you. . . . [Solomon said]
So give Your servant an understanding mind and a hearing
heart to judge Your people, that I may discern between good
and bad.

—1 KINGS 3:5,9A

A friend confessed to me one day, "Instead of seeking God's face, I've been guilty of seeking God's gifts. Too many times I have been more excited about what He does for me than I've been about seeking His face and rejoicing in who He is." She went on to say that she craved the blessings and wonderful things God did in her life. The Lord had used her in praying for the sick and had opened doors for her to minister to people.

We've all known ministers of the gospel who were truly blessed and used by God. We also know some of them who had great downfalls. What happened? I don't know all the details, but I know enough about Satan's tactics that I can explain the pattern.

God raises up servants—godly people who truly desire

to serve Him and help others. They become successful, and perhaps that's when Satan first attacks them. He reminds them of who they are and how greatly God has used them. (Satan sometimes tells the truth to lead to a lie.) He encourages them to become even more successful or famous—whatever their weaknesses, he plays on those.

If they don't rebuke the evil voice, they soon push forward and seek greater spiritual gifts. They want to be the best-known healers in the world or the greatest evangelists. Too often, they don't hear God's quiet voice or sense His sadness as they push forward.

Before long, they want what God gives, but they don't really want God. That's one of Satan's oldest tricks. He tried to accuse God of *bribing* His followers. In the first chapter of Job, God called Job blameless and upright, one who feared God and shunned evil (see Job 1:8b).

"Then Satan answered the Lord, Does Job [reverently] fear God for nothing? Have You not put a hedge about him and his house and all that he has, on every side? You have conferred prosperity and happiness upon him in the work of his hands, and his possessions have increased in the land. But put forth Your hand now and touch all that he has, and he will curse You to Your face" (Job 1:9–11)

Of course, we know that Job didn't give in to the devil. He had truly sought God and not His gifts. The book of Job tells of one hardship and trial after another, including the devil using his friends to plead with him to give up. Job never did quit because he sought God more than he sought His gifts.

By contrast, think of King Saul—Israel's first king. He was tall, handsome, and chosen by God. He could have been a great leader, but he allowed Satan to win the battle over his mind. Later, Saul was so possessed by evil spirits that he needed young David to play his lute to calm the troubled spirit. At the end of his life, Saul went to a witch for an answer because he knew God had departed from him. That's a man who yielded to the devil. He sought gifts and power more than he sought God.

Our heavenly Father delights in giving His children good things—but only if you seek after *Him* first. In the verses above, when Solomon asked for wisdom, God not only gave him wisdom but he commended him for not asking for long life or riches. And because he didn't ask for those things, God said, "I'm going to give them to you anyway." That's the generous way the Lord works. When you seek Him, He gives generously; when you seek only His gifts, you may receive those gifts, but you will also get an empty life. Or worse, you may allow Satan to advance.

———————

Great and all-wise God, forgive me for looking at the wrong things. Help me to seek You, to yearn only for You and how I may please You. I want You to use me to serve You, but most of all, I want to know that my life pleases You. I ask for Your help, in the name of Jesus. Amen.

68

D.V.

*Come now, you who say, Today or tomorrow we will go into
such and such a city and spend a year there and carry on our
business and make money. Yet you do not know [the least
thing] about what may happen tomorrow. . . . You ought
instead to say, If the Lord is willing, we shall live and we
shall do this or that [thing].*

—JAMES 4:13–15

He told me that he and his wife were missionaries to Chad,
Africa, and then he said, "We plan to return in January, *D.V.*"

I didn't know what *D.V.* meant, but I didn't say anything.

As he described his evangelism program for the interior of
the country, he kept saying, "*D.V.*"

Finally, I asked, "What does *D.V.* mean?"

"It's a Latin phrase I learned in school, and it means a great
deal to me," he said. "It stands for *Deo volente,* which means
God willing."

As we talked, I realized how seriously he meant *D.V.* He
said he had great ideas about things he wanted to see happen
in Chad, but more than that, he wanted to be sure his ideas
were in line with God's. "When I say, *D.V.,* that's a reminder to

me—it's my way of saying, 'This is what I'd like. Is it okay with You, Lord?'"

The missionary was totally in line with the words from the book of James, and I loved his humble attitude. He didn't worry about the future, but as he looked ahead, he said, "I like to remind myself that God is the One who decides." He noted that far too many Christians plan their lives by what *they* want to do. It's as if they say, "Okay, God, this is what I'm going to do. I hope You're okay with that."

James calls that boasting! "You boast [falsely] in your presumption and your self-conceit. All such boasting is wrong" (4:16).

God calls us to live—here and now—but to live one day at a time. There are a lot of boasting people out there—they decide what they want and expect everything to run smoothly. That can be a trick of Satan, as well. If he can get them to focus on tomorrow or next year, they don't have to deal with the problems in their lives right now. They can live in a world of only good things that will take place in the future. Isn't that like driving a car down the highway and ignoring what's right in front of us because we're focused on the traffic signal five blocks ahead? We're setting ourselves up for a wreck.

None of us knows what's ahead. We can think and plan, but it's up to God to make those plans happen. Few people seem to know how to live each day to the fullest. That means to live in the now and to enjoy life as it is. If we look ahead, we do so and say, "God, show me Your will so that I don't boast or race ahead of You."

Jesus promised us a life of abundance (see John 10:10). But we can't enter into that abundance if we're not giving our lives fully to Him. Don't spend today planning tomorrow and avoid the issues that confront you now. That is one of Satan's oldest tricks—to plan for tomorrow and to ignore today.

———————

My heavenly Father, please help me live today. Whether I actually say the words *D.V.* or not, remind me that Your will is more important than anything in my life. Help me not to allow Satan to get me thinking so much about tomorrow that I fail to live today in a way that pleases You. I ask this in Jesus' name. Amen.

69

Casting Our Cares upon God

Therefore humble yourselves [demote, lower yourselves in your own estimation] under the mighty hand of God, that in due time He may exalt you, casting the whole of your care [all your anxieties, all your worries, all your concerns, once and for all] on Him, for He cares for you affectionately and cares about you watchfully.

—1 PETER 5:6–7

It is important that we learn to humble ourselves and cast our care on the Lord. We shouldn't struggle to believe that God wants us to lay all of our concerns at the foot of the cross, when He so clearly has told us in His Word to do exactly that.

The word *casting* refers to throwing, hurling, arising, sending, striking, thrusting, driving out, or expelling—all rather forceful terms. It seems to be difficult for some of us to believe that God considers worry or care a sin. So we may actually have to become spiritually violent about casting our care upon the Lord and abiding in the secret place of the Most High, under the shadow of the Almighty.

It literally took me years to be set totally free from the

burden of guilt and condemnation. I knew mentally and spiritually that I had been made the righteousness of God in Christ because of what He had done for me on Calvary, but I still had a hard time accepting it and living in it emotionally. The devil kept attacking my feelings, making me feel guilty and condemned. I worried about my past—how could I ever overcome it? I fought against those thoughts for years until finally I got fed up. I told the devil, "No! I am not going to believe your lies! Jesus has made me the righteousness of God, and I have made up my mind that I am going to have what He died to give me!"

I knew from the Bible that I had been made right with God through the shed blood of His Son, Jesus Christ. I was doing my best to keep my mind set on all that Jesus had sacrificed for me. I confessed scriptures, but the enemy still attacked my mind and my feelings until there arose in me a holy anger that finally set me free.

I became angry enough to rise up against the principalities, powers, and wickedness in high places that tried to keep me from enjoying all the blessings God intended for me. Too often, we get mad at other people when our anger should be directed to the source of the problem—the devil and his demons.

Just as anger at Satan can be a form of righteous violence, so can casting our care on the Lord. We can resist Satan, worry and anxiety, and guilt and condemnation, until we get so fed up that we react with a holy anger. When he tries to force us to carry a burden of care, we can stop him in his tracks and say, "No! I will not carry that care. I am casting it upon the Lord!"

Every one of us has certain spiritual issues that must be settled once and for all. We need to cast on the Lord whatever issues we may have that hinder us from walking in the fullness of joy, peace, and rest the Lord intends for us.

Peter says to cast your cares on God. The Greek word translated *care* in 1 Peter 5:7 means "to draw in different directions; to distract." Why does the devil give us care? His whole purpose is to distract us from our fellowship with God. When the enemy tries to lay problems on us, we have the privilege of taking those problems and casting them on God. If you throw them, God catches them and takes them away. God knows how to wipe away the cares that Satan lays on you.

God has provided two wonderful weapons you can use to overcome the devil's plan. First, you humble yourself, turning yourself totally over to God. Then when the devil tries to burden you with worry or some other heavy load, you cast it on God—who is happy to take it away because He cares for you.

As I've thought about worry, I've also figured out that it's an act of pride on our part. Those who worry still think they can solve their own problems. Isn't that pride? Aren't we saying, "I can work this out by myself"? Those who are proud or full of themselves still think they are strong and can defeat their problems themselves. The truly humble are those who know their weaknesses, but in their weaknesses, they know their strength is in Jesus Christ.

Paul understood that and wrote to the Corinthians: "But He said to me, My grace (My favor and loving-kindness and mercy) is enough for you [sufficient against any danger and enables you to bear the trouble manfully]; for My strength and power are made perfect (fulfilled and completed) and show themselves most effective in [your] weakness. Therefore, I will all the more gladly glory in my weaknesses and infirmities, that the strength and power of Christ (the Messiah) may rest (yes, may pitch a tent over and dwell) upon me!" (2 Corinthians 12:9).

We fail God when we insist on shouldering our burdens instead of giving them to the Lord. Only God can deliver us, and He wants us to know that. In every situation, He wants us to first humble ourselves and then throw off the cares and worries the devil tries to lay on us. It is possible—in fact, it's an order. I want to encourage you to place yourself totally into God's hands and allow Him to be the Manager of your life.

Dear Lord Jesus, I thank You. Even before the problems come, You have told me how to defeat the enemy of my mind. You have also given me Your own example of defeating him. In Your name, Lord Jesus, teach me to humble myself and to cast all my cares and concerns on You. Amen.

70

Holy Fear

Then Jehoshaphat feared, and set himself [determinedly, as his vital need] to seek the Lord; he proclaimed a fast in all Judah. And Judah gathered together to ask help from the Lord; even out of all the cities of Judah they came to seek the Lord [yearning for Him with all their desire]. . . . Did not You, O our God, drive out the inhabitants of this land before Your people Israel and give it forever to the descendants of Abraham Your friend? . . . O our God, will You not exercise judgment upon them? For we have no might to stand against this great company that is coming against us. We do not know what to do, but our eyes are upon You.

—2 CHRONICLES 20:3–4, 7, 12

By the time Jehoshaphat became the king, Judah was a small nation, and the surrounding nations could easily defeat them. We learn that the king brought in many reforms. The Bible records that and then says, "After this, the Moabites, the Ammonites, and with them the Meunites came against Jehoshaphat to battle" (20:1).

The most "sensible" thing would have been for the king to surrender and to forge some kind of treaty. There was no human way that such a small nation could defeat such large armies. In that context, we read that the king was afraid—and why wouldn't he be? But he didn't stop with fear.

I want to make this point clear. To feel fear isn't sin or failure or disobedience. In fact, we do well to think of fear as a warning to us. It's a shout of danger.

But then we must decide what to do with the fear. We can act; we can cringe; we can ignore it. King Jehoshaphat did the right thing: He "set himself [determinedly, as his vital need] to seek the Lord" (v. 3). He didn't have answers, and he certainly wasn't stupid enough to think that his tiny army could defeat his enemies. And that's an important lesson for us to learn in our battles against Satan. Our enemy is powerful, and if we think we can defeat him by ourselves, we're foolish and badly mistaken.

The king not only prayed, but he also proclaimed a fast throughout the entire land. The Bible goes on to say that he stood in the midst of the people and prayed for deliverance: "For we have no might to stand against this great company that is coming against us. We do not know what to do, but our eyes are upon You" (v. 12).

That is exactly the prayer God wanted to hear. The people admitted they didn't know what to do, that they couldn't win, and that their only hope was in God's deliverance.

Just then, the Holy Spirit came upon a man named Jahaziel. "He said, hearken, all Judah, you inhabitants of Jerusalem, and you King Jehoshaphat. The Lord says this to you: Be not afraid or dismayed at this great multitude; for the battle is not yours, but God's" (v. 15). He went on to say, "You shall not need to fight in this battle; take your positions, stand still, and see the deliverance of the Lord [Who is] with you. . . . Fear not nor be dismayed" (v. 17). The account goes on to say that the people began to sing praises to God. When they did that, God had warriors from Mount Seir sneak in and kill Judah's enemies so that none escaped.

That's the biggest secret of winning the battles against your enemy. You acknowledge your fear—you can even call it "holy fear" because it pushes you to seek God. If you're not really afraid (or worried) and don't see the problem as bigger than yourself, why would you call for God's help? But when it becomes overwhelming, you realize that you need divine help. Isaiah says it this way: "When the enemy shall come in like a flood, the Spirit of the Lord will lift up a standard against him and put him to flight [for He will come like a rushing stream which the breath of the Lord drives]" (Isaiah 59:19b).

When you cry out in holy fear, God hears and races to your rescue. That's His promise, and He never breaks His promises to His own.

———————

God, I've known fear, and too often I've concentrated on the fear and forgotten that it's an opportunity to call on You so I can see Your hand of deliverance in my life. Give me holy fear so that I'll always call on You in my times of trouble. In the name of Jesus Christ, I ask this. Amen.

71

Wasted Life

[Jesus said]
Peace I leave with you; My [own] peace I now give and
bequeath to you. Not as the world gives do I give to you. Do
not let your hearts be troubled, neither let them be afraid.
[Stop allowing yourselves to be agitated and disturbed; and
do not permit yourselves to be fearful and intimidated and
cowardly and unsettled].

—JOHN 14:27

I have told you these things, so that in Me you may have
[perfect] peace and confidence. In the world you have
tribulation and trials and distress and frustration; but be of
good cheer [take courage; be confident, certain, undaunted]!
For I have overcome the world. [I have deprived it of power
to harm you and have conquered it for you].

—JOHN 16:33

In my book *Battlefield of the Mind,* I admit: "I wasted many
years of my life worrying about things I could do nothing
about. I would like to have those years back and be able to
approach them in a different way. However, once you have
spent the time God has given you, it is impossible to get it
back and do things another way."[2]

What I didn't realize for so many years was that Jesus'

peace is always there, ready and waiting for us. His peace is spiritual, and His rest operates in the middle of trouble, noise, and confusion. Too often, we think we'd be just fine if there weren't so many storms in life. But that's absolutely not true. Real peace comes from going *through* the storms and winning the battles of life.

I attended the funeral of an elderly gentleman several years ago. Near the casket stood the eighty-four-year-old widow, who had just lost her husband in a fire that had totally destroyed their home. She barely came out alive herself. Just a week or so earlier, her son had died of cancer, and her daughter had been killed in a freakish car accident. She had lost all of her loved ones within a period of two weeks!

"How are you handling all of this?" I heard someone ask her. "How can one person endure so much?"

The woman's eyes were moist as she replied, but her voice was firm. She said, "It wasn't easy. I felt as if I were walking across a river that kept getting deeper, and I was sure I would drown. I kept crying out for God's help. And do you know what? My feet touched the riverbed, and my head was still above the water. I had made it across. God was with me. His peace enabled me to keep going when I was sure I would drown."

This is how God's peace works. Jesus made it clear that we don't have to worry, because He is with us. No matter how deep the water, He is always there.

I thought again of my years of worrying and living without God's peace. I was a Christian, and I tried to follow God in every way I knew. However, money was a big problem in those days, and many times, I wondered if we would be able to pay all of our bills.

My husband, Dave, never seemed to worry about anything. I'd be ready to collapse under the stress of it all, and he'd be in the other room playing and wrestling with the children. One time I asked, in frustration, "Why don't you help me figure this out instead of playing with the children?"

"What would you like me to do?" he asked.

I didn't know what to say. There was nothing he could do, and I knew it, but it upset me that he could go on enjoying life as if we weren't in a desperate financial situation. But that was also a great moment of awakening for me.

I had been at the kitchen table for at least an hour worrying, and fretting, and trying to figure out how to pay all our bills. No matter what I did, we simply didn't have enough money that month. Dave understood the problem and didn't like it any more than I did, but he didn't fret. He knew there was nothing he could do to change the figures.

He didn't say it, but I realized what he meant. "If we can't change anything, why are you wasting your life trying to fix the things that can't be fixed?"

As I look back, I'm ashamed of myself. I wasted so many hours of my early married life. Instead of enjoying my life, my children, and my husband, I wasted my energies on trying to fix things I couldn't fix.

God met our financial needs—sometimes through amazing miracles—and all my worry was for nothing. I wasted a precious time in my life—part of the wonderful, abundant life Jesus offered to me. I have it now, and I'm grateful, but I could have had a more abundant life back then. It took me a while, but I have finally learned to enjoy the faithfulness of my heavenly Father.

———————————

God of all peace, help me to recognize and enjoy Your presence in my life and to be thankful for all Your blessings. Don't let me waste my life worrying about things that only You can control. In the name of Jesus, I ask You to free me from worry. Amen.

Real Problems

Let your character or moral disposition be free from love of
money [including greed, avarice, lust, and craving for
earthly possessions] and be satisfied with your present
[circumstances and with what you have]; for He [God]
Himself has said, I will not in any way fail you nor give you
up nor leave you without support.

—HEBREWS 13:5

I recently heard an interesting story about the difference
between real and imagined problems—something that all of
us have probably faced at one time or another. This story
involved a man who was in his second year of Bible college.
He was faced with financial challenges and couldn't figure
out how to pay his bills, support his family, and remain
in school. He and his wife were expecting their second
child, and because of health problems, she required total bed
rest. He finally made an appointment with the financial aid
office.

He nervously walked in and sat down. Then the man
across the desk asked him an interesting question, "Do you
need money, or do you have real problems?"

That question changed his life. Why? Because he had seen money as his biggest and most-difficult-to-solve problem. His bills and financial needs were constantly on his mind. It was as if his need for money had become the most important thing in his life.

Before this young student could say anything more, the financial counselor smiled and said, "Most of the students come in because they need money. Money becomes the center of their lives, and it steals their victory and peace."

The student felt as if this man had been reading his mail. Until that moment, he had been one of those students the man had described. In his quest to figure out how to make ends meet, victory and peace had completely eluded him.

The wise financial counselor made some very interesting observations that day. He said, "The problem isn't money, son, the problem is trust. We have a few financial loans we can make, but that won't solve your problem. You see, your problem is inside your head and your heart. If you can get those things in the right order, money will no longer be the focus of your life."

No one had ever spoken to him like that before. "Not only did the loan counselor force me to rethink my life and my priorities," the student said, "but he pointed me in the right direction."

The loan counselor pulled out his Bible, and asked the student to read three verses that had been underlined in red and highlighted in yellow. "The steps of a [good] man are directed and established by the Lord when He delights in his way [and He busies Himself with his every step]. Though he falls, he shall not be utterly cast down, for the Lord grasps his hand in support and upholds him. I have been young and now am old, yet have I not seen the [uncompromisingly] righteous forsaken or their seed begging bread" (Psalm 37:23–25).

"So look at yourself, son," the man said. "Are you a good man? Are you a righteous person? If you are, what does that say about you and your relationship with God?"

The student read those verses aloud twice, and recognized that those words were a picture of himself. He had fallen—he had allowed himself to become discouraged—and he had been ready to give up. But he knew he was in Bible college because that's where God wanted him to be.

As he left the financial aid office, he had received no money and no offer for aid, but he left with a lighter heart and an assurance that he would not have to leave school. He was a little slow in paying some of his bills—and a few times, he had to get an extension on paying his tuition—but he was able to stay and complete his education. Today he is in full-time pastoral ministry.

God takes great care of His own, and He will take care of you. Hebrews 13:5 offers you assurance that you don't have to set your mind on money, wondering and worrying how you can take care of yourself. God has promised to take care of you, so what more is there to say?

God of all precious promises, I'm ashamed that I've allowed money or other problems to become so important that I've lost my perspective. My problem isn't money; my problem is my lack of trust in You. As I meditate on Your promises, help me to truly believe that You will perform Your Word in my life. In the name of Jesus Christ, I pray. Amen.

73

The Critical Mind

[Jesus said]
A good (healthy) tree cannot bear bad (worthless) fruit, nor
can a bad (diseased) tree bear excellent fruit [worthy of
admiration]. Every tree that does not bear good fruit is cut
down and cast into the fire. Therefore, you will fully know
them by their fruits.

—Matthew 7:18–20

Have you ever met someone who had "the gift of suspicion"?
They are everywhere—even in church. Recently I heard a
man commenting about such a woman in his church. He said
she always seemed to think the worst of everyone. If someone
did something generous, she would say, "What does he expect to get out of that? I suppose he wants us all to bow and
thank him."

On one occasion, someone commented about what a
friendly, happy person an usher was. "That's his public face,"
the woman said. "He's always smiling, but I'll bet when he gets
home and away from everyone else, he doesn't smile like that."

He went on to say if someone chided her for her critical attitude, the woman only responded by saying, "I just call

things as I see them. You're always trying to make things look better than they are."

The man finally realized that it wasn't good for him to be around her, and he began to distance himself from her as much as possible.

I believe this man made a good decision. I have discovered during my years in ministry that when someone with a critical spirit comes into a group or a meeting, it doesn't take much for others to become infected with it. It reminds me of the saying about one bad apple spoiling the whole bushel.

Over the years, I've met people who were very much like this lady. They're often tormented by their judgmental attitudes, critical spirits, and suspicious minds. They also destroy many relationships by their words.

Matthew 7:18 says these "bad fruits" tell us a lot about the "tree," but that doesn't give us the right to judge. We must remember that no one is perfect—each of us is a work in progress. While it may be wise not to be too closely associated with such people, we must be careful that we don't judge them according to our standards and beliefs. We must pray for them and keep a godly attitude. Part of being a loving, caring Christian is to realize that people may not see things in this life exactly as we do. We are not all at the same level of Christian maturity, but we can be sure that God knows everything about each one of us. We must leave any judging to the only righteous judge—Jesus Christ.

James writes: "[My] brethren, do not speak evil about or accuse one another. He that maligns a brother or judges his brother is maligning and criticizing the Law and judging the Law. But if you judge the Law, you are not a practicer of the Law but a censor and judge [of it]. One only is the Lawgiver and Judge Who is able to save and to destroy [the one Who has the absolute power of life and death]. [But you] who are you that [you presume to] pass judgment on your neighbor?" (James 4:11–12).

Paul asks, "Who are you to pass judgment on and censure another's household servant? It is before his own master that he stands or falls. And he shall stand and be upheld, for the Master (the Lord) is mighty to support him and make him stand" (Romans 14:4).

———————

Dear heavenly Father, forgive me for criticizing others. I know that You are the only one who is qualified to judge Your children. Help me remember that all of us, including me, must give account of ourselves to You—and only to You. Help me, Lord Jesus, to bear good fruit in my own life that will bring glory to You. Amen.

74

"I" Problems

*Now Miriam and Aaron talked against Moses [their brother]
because of his Cushite wife, for he had married a Cushite
woman. And they said, Has the Lord indeed spoken only by
Moses? Has he not spoken also by us?*
—NUMBERS 12:1–2

Moses' sister, Miriam, and his brother, Aaron, complained to
God about the Ethiopian woman their brother had married
during his forty years of exile. But that was not the real issue.
The real problem was revealed when they asked, "Has the
Lord indeed spoken only by Moses? Has he not spoken also
by us?"

That's the big "I" problem—also known as the issue of
pride. That's one way Satan gets into our lives, divides us,
confuses us, and causes us to fight among ourselves.

In the incident cited above, the issue wasn't whether God
spoke through them or only through Moses. It was their way
of calling attention to themselves and yearning for recogni-
tion. But their plan backfired on them. If you read the entire
account, you will find that God punished Miriam with lep-
rosy and she had to stay outside the camp for a week.

There's another interesting note: *She held them back from moving forward.* "So Miriam was shut up without the camp for seven days, and the people did not journey on until Miriam was brought in again" (v. 15).

What we need to recognize about pride—one of Satan's most powerful tools—is that while it may actually attack only one or two of us, it affects everyone. When someone stands up and says, "I am special," the unspoken message is: "But you—you're not special like me." That's when jealousies and anger erupt—and the devil is the only one who is happy.

Here's another example. A few months ago, I saw a brief review of a college football game on the evening news. The running back stood just over the goal line, jumping up and down and screaming, "I'm the best! I'm the best!"

I'm sure he was excited because he had won the game. *Or had he?* What he didn't seem to grasp was that he had only carried the ball over the line, scoring the winning points. His teammates, however, had thrown him the ball and blocked other players from tackling him. His statement would have been more accurate had he said, "*We're* the best!"

This illustrates a dangerous attitude. Much of the time, we are only too eager to take all the credit. Too many people act as if they are solely responsible for their gifts and abilities (see 1 Corinthians 4:7). What they—and all of us—need to realize and focus on is that God alone gives us all of the talents, abilities, and gifts that we need to succeed in life. He is the giver . . . we are just the recipients.

Whenever we excel in any area, it is because God has

equipped us with the necessary abilities. God expects us to utilize our gifts and become better at the things we do, but we must never forget that He is the one who gives the talent. If we're high-minded or think more highly of ourselves than we should, we tend to look down on others. This is the sin of pride, and no one appreciates it. We all back away from proud people because they not only elevate themselves, but they arouse negative feelings in the rest of us, especially if we have any issues of insecurity or inferiority.

To win over the big "I" problem, we must remind ourselves of this simple fact: Everything we are and everything we have comes as a gift from God. If we stay focused on that fact, pride will find no place in our hearts.

———————

Patient and loving God, forgive me when I've taken credit for my talents and my abilities. Help me now and every day to thank You for the gifts and abilities that You have so generously placed in me. I ask this in the name of my Savior, Jesus. Amen.

75

When Someone Fails

*Well then, you who teach others, do you not teach yourself?
While you teach against stealing, do you steal (take what
does not really belong to you)? You who say not to commit
adultery, do you commit adultery [are you unchaste in action
or in thought]? . . . You who boast in the Law, do you
dishonor God by breaking the Law [by stealthily infringing
upon or carelessly neglecting or openly breaking it]? For, as
it is written, the name of God is maligned and blasphemed
among the Gentiles because of you!*

—ROMANS 2:21–24

Paul's words remind me of a saying I used to hear often:
"Don't do as I do—do as I say." The people who give this ad-
monition expect others to live according to rules that they
themselves admittedly are not willing to follow.

This is where many young or insecure Christians find
themselves. They see some church leaders or those in authority doing things they know aren't right, and they think, *Well,
if they're such great Christians and they can do that . . . it must
be all right.* This attitude can either lead them to do the same
things or to turn away from God altogether.

We need to remember that God has called us to be responsible for *our* actions. God holds us accountable for every thought and every action—but our responsibility doesn't stop there. We are also responsible to help lift up others when they fall.

Perhaps nowhere in the Bible is this concept more clearly defined than in Galatians 6:1-3. Paul laid down three important principles that Satan doesn't want us to grasp. First, when we become aware that a sister or brother has fallen into sin, we are to do whatever we can to help lift up that person. Paul wrote, "If any person is overtaken in misconduct or sin of any sort, you who are spiritual [who are responsive to and controlled by the Spirit] should set him right and restore and reinstate him, without any sense of superiority and with all gentleness, keeping an attentive eye on yourself, lest you should be tempted also. Bear (endure, carry) one another's burdens and troublesome moral faults, and in this way fulfill and observe perfectly the law of Christ (the Messiah) and complete what is lacking [in your obedience to it]. For if any person thinks himself to be somebody [too important to condescend to shoulder another's load] when he is nobody [of superiority except in his own estimation], he deceives and deludes and cheats himself."

Even the best of us fail at times, but it is important to note that the word *overtaken* doesn't mean a deliberate, intentional sin. It's as if someone is walking down an icy sidewalk, slips, and falls. That's how the Christian life works—nearly everyone slips sometimes.

What then should be our attitude when this happens? We should offer to help, of course. If someone slips on the ice, don't you naturally rush over to help that person get up? That's a Christian principle. But the enemy wants to make sure that you don't do the right thing. He might even whisper in your ear, "Just don't look in her direction. Ignore her. You are not obligated to help her get up. Why, you don't even know her." It's easy to ignore people in need of help.

The Greek word translated *restores* was once a medical term used by a surgeon to describe medical procedures like removing a growth from a body or setting a broken arm. The goal is not to see that the person gets punished, but that the person gets healed.

The second point Paul made is that when we become aware someone has fallen, instead of pointing fingers and looking down on them, we should look at ourselves. The devil could have tempted us to do the same thing or something else just as bad . . . or even worse. We need to look with compassion on those who fall and remind ourselves, "Except for the grace of God, I could be there."

The third thing is to push away pride in our own achievements. If we think we are more spiritual, we're deceiving ourselves. Proverbs 16:18 gives this warning: "Pride goes before destruction, and a haughty spirit before a fall." We must not compare our achievements with others, but instead ask ourselves, *Have I really done all that I could have done?* Satan is thrilled when we compare ourselves with those who fail and see ourselves as being superior. But when we compare ourselves with the standards Jesus sets for us, we have no cause to be conceited or prideful. Instead, we can be humbly thankful that the Lord is at work in our lives.

Lord Jesus, please remind me to help those who have fallen. Help me to remember that, except for Your grace, I could be the one who failed. But most of all, help me to remember that You are always with me and will help me overcome the evil one. I give You praise for all these things. Amen.

76

Passing Judgment

[Jesus said]
Do not judge and criticize and condemn others, so that you
may not be judged and criticized and condemned yourselves.
For just as you judge and criticize and condemn others, you
will be judged and criticized and condemned, and in
accordance with the measure you [use to] deal out to others,
it will be dealt out again to you.

—MATTHEW 7:1–2

I believe that pointing a finger at someone in judgment is often the way some people cover up their own weaknesses. Their theory seems to be, "Judge others before they have a chance to judge you." I remember a girl in our neighborhood who constantly pointed to obese people and said terrible things about them. She was plump herself, and I often wondered if she criticized others in an effort to keep people from noticing her own weight.

I grew up in a family where judgment and criticism were a part of everyday life. So I became an expert at deciding how other people should live. The devil loves to keep us busy, mentally judging the faults of others. And the shortcomings in other people are often easy to see, especially when we're looking for them.

There was a time when I enjoyed sitting in the mall, observing people as they walked by. I could usually find something wrong with every one of them. I could point out bad hairstyles, out-of-style clothes, and any number of other "problems." When we *choose* to be judgmental, we will find that there is no end to the possibilities.

Notice I used the words "choose to be judgmental," because that's exactly what I did. If anyone had called me a judgmental or critical person, I would have denied it, because I wasn't aware of my negative attitude. I thought I was just giving my innocent opinion. At that time, I wasn't aware that I had a choice about my thoughts.

Another thing I didn't think about then was the uselessness of my opinions. I didn't help anyone by pointing out to my friends what I perceived to be other people's shortcomings. I now know that we can choose the thoughts we want to focus on. We can't always choose the thoughts that come to our minds, but we can decide to let them stay and fester or we can push them aside.

It took me a while, but I eventually learned that when the devil brings those harsh, unkind, judgmental thoughts to us, we can use God's Word to chase them away. There may be no better verse to repeat than Philippians 4:8 to get our thoughts properly centered: ". . . whatever is true, whatever is worthy of reverence and is honorable and seemly, whatever is just, whatever is pure, whatever is lovely and lovable, whatever is kind and winsome and gracious, if there is any virtue and excellence, if there is anything worthy of praise, think on and weigh and take account of these things [fix your minds on them]."

I went through many years of misery because of judging others. I wanted to be able to say that what others did, or how they looked, was none of my business. And, of course, it wasn't—but it took me a long time to replace those negative thoughts with all the good things I had to think about.

During the process, God began to hold me accountable for my critical spirit, pointing me to the words of Paul: "Why do you criticize and pass judgment on your brother? . . . why do you look down upon or despise your brother? For we shall all stand before the judgment seat of God . . . And so each of us shall give an account of himself [give an answer in reference to judgment] to God. Then let us no more criticize and blame and pass judgment on one another, but rather decide and endeavor never to put a stumbling block or an obstacle or a hindrance in the way of a brother" (Romans 14:10, 12–13).

Who are *we*? We're God's people. As Christians, we're part of one family—God's family. And He wants us to love and protect our family members, instead of judging them.

God, so often I've compared myself to others and judged them. I know that's wrong. In the powerful name of Jesus Christ, I ask You to help me defeat every evil, judgmental thought that Satan throws at me. With Your help and through Your Word, I know I can win. Amen.

77

Loving One Another

*Whoever says he is in the Light and [yet] hates his brother
[Christian, born-again child of God his Father] is in darkness
even until now. Whoever loves his brother [believer] abides
(lives) in the Light, and in It or in him there is no occasion for
stumbling or cause for error or sin. But he who hates (detests,
despises) his brother [in Christ] is in darkness and walking
(living) in the dark; he is straying and does not perceive or know
where he is going, because the darkness has blinded his eyes.*

—1 John 2:9–11

*H*ate is an extremely strong and harsh word. Any discussion
among believers about *hating* other Christians would lead most
of them to say, "I don't believe I have ever hated anyone." If we
think about these words of John, however, perhaps he didn't
mean *hate* as we think of it—feeling great hostility or animosity
toward someone. Perhaps our form of hatred today is more like
indifference. We don't really dislike people, but we don't care
enough to help them when they have troubles and problems.

"Most of the loving I see today in the church is based on
convenience," someone told me recently. He went on to say
that we will reach out to others as long as it's convenient or
doesn't demand too much time or effort.

This opens a wide door of opportunity for Satan to separate us from those who most need our love. Jesus commanded us to love each other. In John 13:34–35, He said that people would recognize us as His disciples by our expressions of love toward one another. Perhaps one reason they don't say that about many of today's Christians is because too often we're unwilling to go out of our way to meet the needs of others.

Love is an action verb. If you love others, you do things for them. To hate (in the biblical sense) is to do nothing or to turn away. To make it worse, you judge and criticize others and think, *If they really loved God, they wouldn't be in such a predicament.*

You need to see that if you practice God's "love walk," you not only grow yourself, but you enable others to grow. The devil can't do you much harm if you truly walk in loving relationship with others.

In my book *Battlefield of the Mind,* I shared the story of how I was extremely sick during my fourth pregnancy. When I prayed for healing, God reminded me that I had criticized another woman in our church who was always tired and sick during her pregnancy. Now, here I was in the same circumstances. I realized how wrong I had been and repented. But it took more than repenting—it also became a time of learning for me. God forced me to realize how often I had judged or criticized others because they didn't measure up to the standards I thought they ought to live by.

All of us make mistakes. All of us have weaknesses. God didn't call us to point out those weaknesses to the person (or worse, to someone else), but He did call us to care—to show Christ's love in any way we can. The Bible tells us to be tender-hearted, understanding, and forgiving. That's how we can win over satanic attacks. Paul says it this way: "And do not grieve the Holy Spirit of God [do not offend or vex or sadden Him], by Whom you were sealed (marked, branded as God's own, secured) for the day of redemption (of final deliverance through Christ from evil and the consequences of sin). Let all bitterness and indignation and wrath (passion, rage, bad temper) and resentment (anger, animosity) and quarreling (brawling, clamor, contention) and slander (evil-speaking, abusive or blasphemous language) be banished from you, with all malice (spite, ill will, or baseness of any kind). And become useful and helpful and kind to one another, tenderhearted (compassionate, understanding, loving-hearted), forgiving one another [readily and freely], as God in Christ forgave you" (Ephesians 4:30–32).

God used these verses to help me see that being Jesus' disciple means being kind to others, tenderhearted, and forgiving. I also realized it meant overlooking their weaknesses and shortcomings. If we truly love others as Christ loves us, it isn't difficult at all.

Lord Jesus, I want to love others, and I want to be kind and caring. I also know that I fail at times. In Your name, I ask You to forgive me, and enable me to forgive others who hurt me or don't live up to my standards. Amen.

78

Guarding Our Hearts

*Keep and guard your heart with all vigilance and above all
that you guard, for out of it flow the springs of life.*
—Proverbs 4:23

*Do not fret or have any anxiety about anything, but in every
circumstance and in everything, by prayer and petition
(definite requests), with thanksgiving, continue to make your
wants known to God. And God's peace . . . which transcends
all understanding shall garrison and mount guard over your
hearts and minds in Christ Jesus.*
—Philippians 4:6–7

I like to connect the verse from Proverbs with Paul's words to
the Philippians. We read that God tells us to guard our
hearts—to watch over them carefully. But what does that really
mean? It means to be alert or watchful about the ways of the
enemy. It's easy to become careless about guarding our hearts
and being alert to Satan's subtle tactics when things are going
our way and God is pouring out His blessings on our lives.

All of us face struggles from time to time, but when we
diligently stand guard over our hearts, we become more
aware that God's plan is for us to overcome.

Instead of using the word *guard,* I like to think of it this way: We need to post a sentinel around our hearts or, as it says above, "garrison and mount guard." Think of what a guard or sentinel does—he's on duty. He watches for the enemy to attack. He's not just ready; he's actively watchful and prepared to resist all attacks from the enemy.

That's how we need to live—with a trustworthy sentinel. It doesn't mean we live in fear or constantly have to check to see if the devil is sneaking around. Think of it more as posting a sentinel to do that for us.

What kind of sentinel do we need? I think of the two most obvious ones: prayer and the Word of God. If we pray for God's Holy Spirit to guard our hearts, He will honor that request. When the enemy creeps up, the sentinel calls out, "Thus saith the Lord," and the enemy flees. (The devil really is a coward and won't openly fight us.)

Read Paul's words again. If we push away our anxieties (which we do by prayer and supplication) and fill our heart with thanksgiving, God's peace stands guard over us. God helps us resist any charge of the enemy.

We also must not minimize thanksgiving. That's such a simple way to keep ourselves alert to Satan's devices. As we give thanks to God through our words and our songs, we are guarding our hearts. As the old hymn says: "Count your blessings— name them one by one; count your many blessings—see what God has done."[3]

It's more than just singing a few words, however—it is actually pausing on purpose to remember all the good things that God has done in our lives. As we rejoice over past blessings, we open ourselves to more blessings in the future.

Another ally we sometimes overlook is other believers. When we're aware of our weaknesses, we can agree in prayer with other believers. We can ask them to pray specifically that we won't be misled or attacked by the enemy when we're not as alert as we should be. Other believers can intercede for us—just as we can for them. What better guards can we post than those who cry out to God on behalf of others? The devil doesn't like hearing such prayers.

———————

Holy Spirit, I ask You to help me be alert against any attack of the enemy by posting the sentinels of prayer and Your Word at the door of my heart. I praise You for showing me how to guard my heart, and pray that I will have a continuously thankful heart. Amen.

79

Suspicious of Suspicion

Love endures long and is patient and kind; love never is
envious nor boils over with jealousy, is not boastful or
vainglorious . . . it is not rude (unmannerly) and does not act
unbecomingly. Love (God's love in us) does not insist on its
own rights or its own way, for it is not self-seeking; it is not
touchy or fretful or resentful; it takes no account of the evil
done to it . . . does not rejoice at injustice and unrighteous-
ness, but rejoices when right and truth prevail. Love bears up
under anything and everything that comes, is ever ready to
believe the best of every person, its hopes are fadeless under
all circumstances, and it endures everything. . . . Love never
fails [never fades out or becomes obsolete or comes to an end].
—1 CORINTHIANS 13:4–8 (A)

These words about love are familiar to most of us, but I can
honestly say that living them has not always been easy for
me. As a child, I was not exposed to this kind of love—in fact,
I was taught to be suspicious of everyone. I was told that the
motives of other people were not to be trusted.

As I got older, I encountered people whose actions con-
firmed in my mind that my suspicions were justified. Even as
a young Christian, I experienced disappointment because of

the obvious motives of some people in the church. While it is wise to be aware of people's motives, we must be careful that we don't allow our suspicious nature to negatively affect our feelings about everyone.

An overly suspicious nature can poison your mind and affect your ability to love and accept other people. Consider this example.

Suppose a friend approaches you after a church service, and says, "Do you know what Doris thinks about you?" Then this friend tells you every detail of the things Doris said. The first problem is that a true friend wouldn't share such information. And the second problem is that with an already suspicious mind, you now believe secondhand information.

Once your mind has been poisoned against someone, suspicion grows. That's when Satan gains a stronghold in your mind. Every time Doris says something to you, you are automatically suspicious, thinking, *What does she really mean?* Or if she's nice to you, you think, *I wonder what she wants from me.*

That's how Satan works. If he can make you suspicious of others, it isn't long before you don't trust anything they say. And if you've been hurt like this several times, the devil can poison your thinking to the point that you start wondering who else may be talking about you behind your back.

Let's continue the example. Suppose that one day in church, Doris is sitting just a few rows in front of you, clapping her hands and praising the Lord. Immediately you think, *She's such a hypocrite.*

Then the Holy Spirit directs your thoughts to your own

condition, and the fact that you were clapping and praising the Lord while harboring bad feelings toward Doris. Didn't Jesus tell us to make peace with others before we present our gifts to Him? (see Matthew 5:24).

Convicted by these words of Jesus, suppose you step forward and apologize to Doris for the bad feelings you have toward her . . . and she stares at you in absolute shock. Then you realize your mistake. You misinterpreted the information your friend had shared with you about Doris, allowing the devil to turn you against a wonderful, godly woman.

This is a good example of how suspicion can cripple relationships and destroy our joy while it leads us astray. This is why learning to develop a 1 Corinthians 13 kind of love is so important.

It took me a while to overcome a lifetime of suspicions, but I finally learned that when we love God's way, we have no place for suspicion of others.

———————

Lord, I thank You for showing me how to overcome my suspicious nature by teaching me how to love others with Your kind of love. Thank You, Jesus, for being patient with me and for being my great example. Amen.

80

Trust God Completely

*But when He was in Jerusalem during the Passover Feast,
many believed in His name [identified themselves with His
party] after seeing His signs (wonders, miracles) which He
was doing. But Jesus [for His part] did not trust Himself to
them, because He knew all [men]; and He did not need
anyone to bear witness concerning man [needed no evidence
from anyone about men], for He Himself knew what was in
human nature. [He could read men's hearts].*

—JOHN 2:23–25

How deeply can we trust others? How much of ourselves do
we give to others, and how vulnerable are we to them? I suppose the answers to these questions are as varied as the different situations. But considering the questions is definitely
food for thought.

Those of us who have been hurt by trusting too much tend
to pull back when we get into certain situations. I was once
involved with a group of women whom I dearly loved, but
eventually I realized our relationship wasn't healthy for them
or for me. I had become too dependent on them, even placing
a trust in them that belongs only to God.

All of us know we're supposed to place our ultimate trust only in the Lord. But sometimes we encounter individuals or groups who mean so much to us that we give too much of ourselves, or we allow them authority in our lives that belongs only to the Lord. When this happens, our lives are out of balance. And when we get out of balance, we open a door for the devil.

The words from John's gospel serve as an appropriate warning to us. He was speaking of the relationship Jesus had with His own beloved disciples. Jesus knew how much—and how little—He could trust even those who were closest to Him. He understood human nature—something all of us have.

Jesus knew that we, too, would need discernment about trusting others, so He sent His Holy Spirit to guide us and to let us know who we could trust. In 1 Corinthians 12:10, the apostle Paul referred to the spiritual gift called the discerning of spirits, and in verse 31, he urged us to "earnestly desire and zealously cultivate the greatest and best gifts . . ." One of these "great gifts" is discernment, and it helps us distinguish between good and bad, not just bad.

True spiritual discernment motivates us to pray when a problem is identified. A genuine problem being discerned by a genuine gift will follow the scriptural plan for dealing with it, not fleshly ways that only exaggerate the problem. As we walk closely with God and ask for His guidance, the Spirit will provide it.

As I mentioned earlier, some seem to have the "gift" of suspicion, and it comes out of an unrenewed mind. Discernment, on the other hand, is the fruit of a renewed spirit.

The book of Acts provides a good example of the discernment and trust issue. The Scriptures describe a couple named Ananias and Sapphira, who were members of the first church in Jerusalem. In those days, believers sold their possessions and shared them with others. This couple sold some land, kept part of the money, and brought the remainder to Peter. That was all right, because it was their money. But only giving part of the money and then leading Peter to believe it was all they had earned from the sale of their property, was not all right.

"But Peter said, Ananias, why has Satan filled your heart that you should lie to and attempt to deceive the Holy Spirit, and should [in violation of your promise] withdraw secretly and appropriate to your own use part of the price from the sale of the land?" (Acts 5:3). Peter pointed out that it was their land and their money. Their sin was in giving only part of the money and claiming it was everything. "You have not [simply] lied to men [playing false and showing yourself utterly deceitful] but to God" (v. 4b).

Both the husband and wife died for that deception. As terrible as that story is, it shows us clearly that the Holy Spirit knows our hearts. And it also shows us that the Spirit can show the intent of our hearts to faithful, committed servants such as Peter through discernment.

God wants us to love and trust others, but we need discernment to guide us. There is a line where our trust and commitment must be reserved only for the Lord. When we give that trust to others, not only will we be disappointed—for no human can live up to our expectations—but we disappoint God.

So don't make that mistake. It is wise to use discernment in loving and trusting others, but you will never go wrong by loving and trusting God completely.

———————

Lord, I trust You, but I want to trust You even more. When I'm tempted to give the trust to others that only You deserve, please help me to be true to You. Help me, through Jesus Christ, to be sensitive to the leading of Your Holy Spirit. Amen.

81

Pleasant Words, Healing Words

*The mind of the wise instructs his mouth, and adds learning
and persuasiveness to his lips. Pleasant words are as a
honeycomb, sweet to the mind and healing to the body.*
—Proverbs 16:23–24

Our thoughts can either get us into trouble or elevate us
above our problems. Too often, however, we allow our minds
to linger over and ponder the wrong kind of thoughts. In the
verse above, it says the mind (or the heart) of the wise
teaches his mouth. This proverb means that the thoughts on
which we dwell will eventually come out in our words. If our
words are good and uplifting, they encourage others and us.

Those thoughts aren't just about others—they are also
about how we reflect on ourselves, as well. One of the smartest
friends I had in school confessed one day that she felt intellec-
tually inferior. Her words shocked me, and I told her so. I
learned that her father used to call her stupid when she didn't
grasp something the first time he explained it to her. Eventually, her own thoughts said to her, *You aren't intelligent enough
to understand this.*

That's a good example of how our words can tear down

others. But we can also uplift others with our words. When we focus on the good, we see in people and tell them, we may well be God's messenger to them.

For example, I've stood in front of a crowd and spoken many times. Because I have victory, they assume I'm always in victory, and that I never have to struggle the way they do. Sometimes a person will come to me and say, "Joyce, God really used you tonight. I came here discouraged and kept asking God what I should do. Right in the middle of your teaching, I heard God speak through you."

Those are pleasant words—as sweet as a honeycomb. Those people who speak to me are often unaware of how hard I've fought the enemy and struggled to free my mind from his influence. When they tell me what a blessing I've been to them, they often don't sense how much their words mean to me.

Everyone needs to hear pleasant and healing words. It's too easy to assume certain people don't have the same struggles or severe battles that we experience. All of us struggle, and for some, it's worse than for others. I believe that the more God wants to use us, the more forcefully Satan exerts his power against us.

We can help each other. When we sincerely speak pleasant words, healing words, we are not only diffusing our enemy's power, but we are building up one another. We need to build up others as much as we need others to encourage us.

I can remember times when I've wanted to say a kind word to someone, and I would think, *Oh, she knows that. She's heard that before.* Then I would say to myself, *Yes, maybe she knows, and perhaps she's heard it before, but she hasn't heard it from me.* It's not that my words are better than anyone else's, but it is the Holy Spirit who takes our words, anoints them, and brings healing and help to others.

What if each of us decided, *I am God's servant to bring healing words to wounded and hurting hearts*? What if God chose us to strengthen and build up people by speaking soothing, kind, and thoughtful words to them? Not only do we put the devil to flight, but our friends' joy soars, and ours does, too— because we've been used as God's instruments of healing. I learned long ago that it takes so little to do so much good. Often it's only a word of encouragement, a hug, or just saying the words, "I care."

Holy Spirit of God, please remind me of the words that dwell inside me. Remind me to hold on to the good, the kind, and the uplifting thoughts, and empower me to push away those that can hurt and tear down others— and myself. I ask this through Jesus Christ. Amen.

82

Passive Minds

Leave no [such] room or foothold for the devil [give no opportunity to him].

—EPHESIANS 4:27

Perhaps the best way to interpret these words of the apostle Paul is to say it this way: Don't give the devil an opportunity. There are many ways we actually give the devil an opening to pounce on us. One of those ways involves being passive.

To be passive is the opposite of being active. This can be a dangerous problem because it means you aren't on guard, you aren't actively standing up, and you aren't alert. One of the devil's most deceiving tricks is to get you to do nothing and to feel content about it.

I have found a wide variety of definitions for the word *passive,* but I describe it as a lack of feeling, a lack of desire, apathy, laziness, and lukewarmness. It is what John referred to when he wrote to the church at Laodicea: "I know your [record of] works and what you are doing; you are neither cold nor hot. Would that you were cold or hot!" (Revelation 3:15).

It reminds me of something someone told me years ago.

"I've been a good Christian today," he said. "I haven't hurt anyone or done anyone any harm."

In a moment of insight, I said, "But have you done any good for anyone?"

He stared at me for several seconds before he said, "I guess I never thought of it that way. I was so concerned about not doing anything wrong, that I never thought about doing anything good."

That's one of the tricks the devil plays on our minds. All we need to do is read the Bible to find out what God says. Paul wrote to Timothy: "That is why I would remind you to stir up (rekindle the embers of, fan the flame of, and keep burning) the [gracious] gift of God [the inner fire] that is in you by means of the laying on of my hands [with those of the elders at your ordination]. For God did not give us a spirit of timidity (of cowardice, of craven and cringing and fawning fear), but [He has given us a spirit] of power and of love and of calm and well-balanced mind and discipline and self-control" (2 Timothy 1:6–7). Paul told his young disciple to shake himself up and do something—which is good for us to consider, as well. Paul urged us to get moving and start using the gifts God has given us.

The devil knows that inactivity, laziness, or failure to exercise our will for doing good can throw us into ultimate defeat. As long as we move against the devil, we can win the battle. When we do nothing, we become his prime target. It's when we get stirred into action, and passionate about faith, and zealous to follow God that we can destroy all the devil's influence.

Peter wrote to the persecuted believers of his day: "Be well balanced (temperate, sober of mind), be vigilant and cautious at all times; for that enemy of yours, the devil, roams around like a lion roaring [in fierce hunger], seeking someone to seize upon and devour. Withstand him; be firm in faith [against his onset—rooted, established, strong, immovable, and determined]" (1 Peter 5:8–9a).

I stress this because I see many believers who don't feel passionate about anything, so they don't do anything. They attend worship services and praise the Lord if they feel like it. They read their Bibles if they have the energy and time. If they don't feel like doing something, they just don't do it.

That's not God's way. We need to stir ourselves up—the way Paul urged Timothy. I'll use myself as an example to illustrate what I mean. I don't really enjoy physical exercise that much, but the more I exercise, the easier it gets and the better I feel. It was pretty tough when I first started the program. In fact, it hurt. I was sore. I ached all over, and I wanted to quit. I'd been so inactive (passive) for so long about physical exercise that it was painful! And my physical condition only worsened as long as I did nothing about it. But exercising consistently eventually paid off.

Let me encourage you to stir yourself. Get active. You don't want to give place to the devil by doing nothing. If you make the effort to praise and to read the Bible, you give God the opportunity to bless you. If you don't make the effort, you are inviting the enemy into your life. Get moving! Start today.

God, help me to stir myself up, especially on those days when I don't feel passionate. Help me remember that it is an act of the will that You honor. In the name of Jesus, help me to stay vigilant and active—and that means being victorious, as well. Amen.

83

Overcoming Passivity

> *[Jesus said]*
> *When the unclean spirit has gone out of a person, it roams*
> *through waterless places in search [of a place] of rest*
> *(release, refreshment, ease); and finding none it says, I will*
> *go back to my house from which I came. And when it arrives,*
> *it finds [the place] swept and put in order and furnished and*
> *decorated. And it goes and brings other spirits, seven [of*
> *them], more evil than itself, and they enter in, settle down,*
> *and dwell there; and the last state of that person is worse*
> *than the first.*
>
> —Luke 11:24–26

This word from Jesus can be frightening. His purpose for the warning is not to cause us to cringe and worry about unclean spirits coming back. It's a warning to tell us that it's not enough to get rid of wrong thoughts—we must keep the door locked so our enemy can't return. Not only does evil come back, but it comes back worse than before.

I once read an article about diets, and the author said that most people who diet actually lose weight—until they stop dieting. Then they regain the weight they lost and about 5 percent more. When they stop working at the problem, they not only stop losing, but they're worse than before they started. The author went on to say that the only way to win the battle of being overweight is to make a lifestyle change— by becoming aware of the danger areas and guarding ourselves against making wrong choices.

It works that way spiritually, as well. One way to keep wrong thoughts out of your mind is to keep the mind active and alert and full of right things. You can cast out the devil, but then you must remain alert, always aware of his tricks.

As I point out in my book *Battlefield of the Mind,* there are aggressive sins (or sins of commission) and there are passive sins (sins of omission).[4] That is, there are things we do that hurt a relationship, such as speaking careless words. But it is just as true that we hurt relationships by the omission of kind words, those thoughtful words that express appreciation, affection, or awareness of kind deeds others have done.

When confronted, passive individuals yell, "But I didn't do anything!" That's exactly the point. It's what they don't do. Their lack of action actually invites the devil back into their lives.

That's a strong statement, so I will say it a different way. You can win any time you take action and push away the thoughts and desires that don't come from God. You may do this on your own through prayer, reading the Bible, or even by resisting the passivity that may be natural for you. But once you've been set free, that's only the beginning. It's not just one victory that lasts forever. It's an ongoing battle—it's constantly rebuking the devil.

The best, easiest, and most effective way to rebuke the devil is to fill your mind and your heart with praises to God. When you worship and praise God, you've slammed the door in the enemy's face and put up a "No Trespassing" sign.

I don't want to make it sound as if you have to fight demons every second of your life. That's a trick of the devil himself to make you think like that. But when you fill your life with praise and positive, healthy thoughts, you can live in victory.

Please read this verse again—aloud—and hear the message of the Holy Spirit: "Finally, my friends, keep your minds on whatever is true, pure, right, holy, friendly, and proper. Don't ever stop thinking about what is truly worthwhile and worthy of praise" (Philippians 4:8 CEV).

Victory over passivity is just that simple: Focus your mind on the good and you will have no space left for the passive or the bad.

God, thank You for showing me the way to win over passivity and live in victory every day. In the name of Jesus, I ask You to remind me each day so that I can fill my mind and heart with only worthy thoughts. Amen.

84

Right Action Follows Right Thinking

*Do not be conformed to this world (this age) [fashioned after
and adapted to its external, superficial customs], but be
transformed (changed) by the [entire] renewal of your mind
[by its new ideals and its new attitude], so that you may
prove [for yourselves] what is the good and acceptable and
perfect will of God, even the thing which is good and
acceptable and perfect [in His sight for you].*

—ROMANS 12:2

A friend once talked about a church building their congregation had bought. "Function follows form," he said, as he explained that the shape of the building and the size of the rooms
had already determined how they could best use the building.

As I thought about it, I realized that's exactly how our lives
work. Once we decide the form, the function follows. This
could be stated another way by saying, once we set our minds
to something—that's the form—the function, or the action,
follows.

Too many people want to change their actions but not
their thoughts. They want to be free from anger, gossip, lust,
dishonesty, or lying. They want the bad behavior to stop, but
they don't want to change their bad thinking.

The principle of God's Word is simple: Right action follows right thinking. None of us ever walks in victory unless we understand and put this principle into practice. We won't change our behavior until we change our way of thinking.

Many people struggle over trying to do the right thing. One woman told me that she had been a real gossip—not that her words were always evil, but she just liked to talk. It was as if she felt compelled to be the first person to know anything and then to pass it on as quickly as possible. She struggled with holding back or saying less, and it didn't work.

My advice to her was, "Until you change your way of thinking, you won't be free." Then I said I would be glad to pray for her, but added, "You must be accountable."

"I am—and I will be—" she interrupted.

"No, you haven't heard me. You want deliverance from all the gossip, but you don't want to make any changes in your thinking. It just doesn't work that way. You need deliverance in your mind; then your words and actions will change."

She resisted my words, but she did ask me to pray for her, which I did. When I finished, she began to cry. "As you prayed, I understood. God showed me how insignificant and unimportant I feel. When I'm the first to pass on information, it makes me feel good—at least for a while—and important."

She had been asking us to pray for her to change her behavior, but she still wanted to feel good about what she did. She had to shift her thinking and learn to accept that she was worthwhile and loved by God just for being who she was. Once she learned to change her way of thinking—and she did over a course of weeks—she no longer had a problem with her tongue.

It's impossible to change wrong behavior to right behavior without an attitude adjustment, which means that first we change the way we think. .

I like the way Paul taught in Ephesians 4. He contrasted the old nature with the renewed mind. He admonished his readers: "Strip yourselves of your former nature [put off and discard your old unrenewed self] which characterized your previous manner of life and becomes corrupt through lusts and desires that spring from delusion; And be constantly renewed in the spirit of your mind [having a fresh mental and spiritual attitude], and put on the new nature (the regenerate self) created in God's image, [Godlike] in true righteousness and holiness (4:22–24).

Another translation puts it this way: "Let the Spirit change your way of thinking, and make you into a new person. You were created to be like God, and so you must please him and be truly holy" (4:23–24 CEV).

There it is: Let the Holy Spirit change your way of thinking. That's the only way you can make permanent changes in your life.

———————

Holy Spirit, thank You for Your ability to help me change my thinking. Help me strip myself of the old ways of thinking so that You can work in me to make me more like Jesus Christ. It's in His name that I pray. Amen.

85

The Mind of Christ

For who has known or understood the mind (the counsels and purposes) of the Lord so as to guide and instruct Him and give Him knowledge? But we have the mind of Christ (the Messiah) and do hold the thoughts (feelings and purposes) of His heart.

—1 Corinthians 2:16

This verse overwhelms many people. If these were not the words of the Bible, they wouldn't believe it. As it is, most people shake their heads and ask, "How can this be?"

Paul was not saying we're perfect or that we'll never fail. He was telling us, as believers in Jesus, the Son of God, we are given the mind of Christ. That is, we can think spiritual thoughts because Christ is alive within us. We no longer think the way we once did. We begin to think as He did.

Another way to look at this is to point to the promise God spoke through Ezekiel: "A new heart will I give you and a new spirit will I put within you, and I will take away the stony heart out of your flesh and give you a heart of flesh. And I will put my Spirit within you and cause you to walk in My statutes, and you shall heed My ordinances and do them.

And you shall dwell in the land that I gave to your fathers; and you shall be My people, and I will be your God" (Ezekiel 36:26–28).

God gave that promise through the prophet when the Jews were in exile in Babylon. He wanted to show them that their present situation was not the end. They had sinned and failed Him in every conceivable way, but He would not abandon them. Instead, He would change them. He would give them a new spirit—His Holy Spirit.

When we have the Holy Spirit living and active within us, the mind of Christ is in action. The mind of Christ is given to us to direct us in the right way. If we have His mind, we will think positive thoughts. We will think about how blessed we are—how good God has been to us. I realize I've already written about the importance of being positive, but I'm not sure that enough can ever be said about the power of being positive.

Jesus was positive, in spite of being lied about, lonely, misunderstood, and a multitude of other negative things. He was deserted by His disciples when He needed them most, yet He remained positive—always able to offer an uplifting, encouraging word. Just being in His presence would suggest that all fear, negative thoughts, and discouraging hopelessness would evaporate into thin air.

The mind of Christ in us is positive. So when we fall for the opportunity to be negative about something, we should instantly discern that we are not operating with the mind of Christ. God wants us to be lifted up. It's the enemy of our soul who wants us pressed down—depressed. Except for a medical reason, I do not think it is possible to be depressed without being negative. We have many opportunities to think negative thoughts, but that is not the mind of Christ at work in us. We don't have to accept those thoughts. They are not ours!

Every situation that presents itself gives us an opportunity to make a choice. It's obvious, of course, that we can choose the good or the bad.

What we often forget is that we choose the bad or the wrong without conscious thought. We follow old patterns—or the old mind—and not the mind of Christ. As God promised the Jews through Ezekiel's prophecy, He will give us a new heart and a new spirit, but we still have the power to choose which mind we want to follow.

———————

Lord, I truly want to be aware of the mind of Christ in my life, and I want to be aware of it every minute of my waking day. Help me to open myself only to Your will and to push away the old mindsets, the thinking that will lead me down the wrong path. I ask this through Jesus Christ. Amen.

86

Go with God's Flow

*Now the mind of the flesh [which is sense and reason
without the Holy Spirit] is death [death that comprises
all the miseries arising from sin, both here and hereafter].
But the mind of the [Holy] Spirit is life and [soul] peace
[both now and forever]. [That is] because the mind of the
flesh [with its carnal thoughts and purposes] is hostile to
God, for it does not submit itself to God's Law; indeed it
cannot. So then those who are living the life of the flesh
[catering to the appetites and impulses of their carnal
nature] cannot please or satisfy God, or be acceptable to
Him. But you are not living the life of the flesh, you are
living the life of the Spirit, if the [Holy] Spirit of God [really]
dwells wihin you [directs and controls you].*

—ROMANS 8:6–9A

God's Word makes it clear. If you follow the carnal mind—
the natural, unregenerated mind—it leads to death. But if
you are spiritually minded, which means the Spirit of God
lives in you and you heed what He tells you to do, you are
alive and you walk with God.

The choice is yours. You can travel down the river of least
resistance and let the undertow pull you wherever it wants.

Or you can choose to go with God's flow. We call that walking in the Spirit, or living the mind of Christ.

I have several suggestions for teaching you how to flow in the mind of Christ. The first is to develop positive thoughts. For many people, that doesn't happen naturally. It's easy for your mind to sink to the lowest level and think the worst of people. Instead, you can train yourself to think positively. "Do two walk together except they make an appointment and have agreed?" asks Amos 3:3. If you walk with Christ, you can think Christ-like thoughts. You can see the good in others and lift them up.

Think of Jesus, who was betrayed by His disciple Judas, was lied about by the priests, and was denied by Peter—yet He never turned negative or bitter. He was always the One who said to people, "Go on your way and from now on sin no more" (John 8:11). In the midst of those voices that cried out, "Crucify him," He prayed, "Father, forgive them, for they know not what they do" (Luke 23:34a).

Because the mind of Christ is positive, whenever your thoughts turn negative, you can be sure you are not going with God's flow. You're not operating by God's power or His Spirit.

Think of it this way: God wants to lift you up and help you focus upward toward the heavens; the devil wants to press you down so you'll focus downward toward the earth.

A second thing you can do is to remind yourself that you are loved. Jesus loved you so much that He died for you—*for you*. "Beloved, let us love one another, for love is (springs) from God; and he who loves [his fellowmen] is begotten (born) of God and is coming [progressively] to know and understand God [to perceive and recognize and get a better and clearer knowledge of Him]. . . . In this is love: not that we loved God, but that He loved us" (1 John 4:7, 10).

Sometimes you may need to say to yourself, *I am loved. God loves me because He created me.* There is an old saying: "God never created any junk," and that means that everything He created was good—including you. If you focus your thoughts on God's love, you will never go astray.

When I first began Joyce Meyer Ministries, God told me to teach the people that He loves them. Too often, we miss this obvious message in the Bible. We look at our imperfections and ask, "How could God possibly love me?" God looks at each of us through eyes of pure love and asks, "How could I not love you? You are mine."

No matter how often you have failed or how weak you are, God holds out to you the wonderful assurance in the words of Paul: "For I am persuaded beyond doubt (am sure) that neither death nor life, nor angels nor principalities, nor things impending and threatening nor things to come, nor powers, nor height nor depth, nor anything else in all creation will be able to separate us from the love of God which is in Christ Jesus our Lord" (Romans 8:38–39).

That's the message: Nothing can separate you from God's love. The more you meditate on God's love for you, the more easily you will flow in His love.

God, I want to walk as close to You as I possibly can. Help me keep my mind on healthy, positive things. Remind me that I am loved—totally and completely loved—by You, and help me to go with Your flow. In Jesus' name, I pray. Amen.

87

Fear Not!

There is no fear in love [dread does not exist], but full-grown (complete, perfect) love turns fear out of doors and expels every trace of terror!
—1 JOHN 4:18

But God shows and clearly proves His [own] love for us by the fact that while we were still sinners, Christ (the Messiah, the Anointed one) died for us.
—ROMANS 5:8

Wouldn't everything in life be better if we didn't have to deal with fear? Of course, there are healthy fears that alert us to danger—and these are good because they protect us. There is also the fear of God, which means to have a holy, reverential awe and respect for Him. But there is a debilitating fear that Satan tries to put on us every day that is intended to keep us from having the power, love, and sound mind that God wants us to have.

If you have ever struggled as I once did with anxiety, you are familiar with the worry, stress, and feeling of heaviness that comes with it. Many people struggle with fear that has no obvious cause or source. They wonder why they are always afraid and can't change, no matter how hard they try.

Others spend every minute worrying about what *might* happen. "What if . . ." is their favorite phrase. "What if I can't pay the bills?" "What if my child gets hurt?" "What if my husband loses his job?" The endless list of possible tragedies keeps these unfortunate people bound up and miserable every day of their lives.

There are many serious things going on in the world, and we need to be aware of them and prepare for them. But we also need to learn to resist fear when it rises up against us. The Word tells us, "God did not give us a spirit of timidity (of cowardice, of craven and cringing and fawning fear), but [He has given us a spirit] of power and of love and of calm and well-balanced mind and discipline and self-control" (2 Timothy 1:7).

Sometimes we think of fear as an emotion, but we need to realize that fear is actually a spirit. In fact, I believe fear is one of Satan's favorite tools, and he particularly loves to torment Christians with it. At every possible opportunity, he will whisper in your ear, telling you that God has forgotten you and there is no hope. It makes sense that Satan would try to intimidate us with fear.

But Jesus said, "All things can be (are possible) to him who believes!" (Mark 9:23). We have to believe that there is nothing worse for the enemy than an on-fire, Bible-believing Christian who is *fearless!* God didn't promise us that life would be easy. We all will face problems and challenges. But the outcome depends on whether we trust God—or give in to fear.

Psalm 23:4 says, "Yes, though I walk through the [deep, sunless] valley of the shadow of death, I will fear or dread no evil, for You are with me; Your rod [to protect] and Your staff [to guide], they comfort me." The psalmist David said he walked *through* the valley.

When we fear or become afraid, we can be sure that's not God at work, but one of the sly tricks of our spiritual enemy. If he can make us think that God hates us or wants to punish us, we'll allow those thoughts to fill our minds, and we'll start losing the battle.

God is love. We can never say those words enough. The only thing we can add is: and God loves me. Fear is a spirit that must be confronted head on—it will not leave on its own. We must proclaim the Word of God and command fear to leave. So the next time fear knocks on your door, send faith to answer!

———————————

Lord Jesus, when I read Your Word, I find assurances of Your love for me. There are times, however, when I feel unworthy of Your love, but You never loved me because I'm worthy; You loved me because You are love. In Your name I pray, Lord Jesus, thanking You for Your reassurance that I am truly loved by You, and that therefore I have no reason to fear. Amen.

88

Be Thankful—Always

Thank [God] in everything [no matter what the circum-
stances may be, be thankful and give thanks], for this is the
will of God for you [who are] in Christ Jesus [the Revealer
and Mediator of that will].

—1 THESSALONIANS 5:18

Someone once told me there are more exhortations in the Bible to praise God than there are of any other kind. I don't know if that's true, but it ought to be. When our minds flow with thanksgiving and praise, we develop immunity to the devil's infectious ways.

If we complain or grumble, the opposite is true. The more we complain, the worse life gets, the more victorious the devil becomes, and the more defeated we feel.

If we are going to live in victory, praise has to be one of our major weapons. A wise pastor once told me, "Praise fills the heaven and the earth with God's presence and drives away the darkness. So if you want to live in the sunshine, praise the Lord."

When good things happen to us, most of us turn to praise. It's easy to lift our hands and our voices when God answers our prayers and delivers us from problems. But it's not always as easy when things go wrong. What do we do when we're sick or lose our jobs or people talk against us? How do we fill our minds with joyful thanksgiving in those situations?

If we read the verse above and add Philippians 4:4: "Rejoice in the Lord always [delight, gladden yourselves in Him]; again I say, Rejoice!" we have options.

The negative option is to take the attitude of Job's wife, who was so shaken up by the loss of her children and their possessions that she cried out, "Do you still hold fast your blameless uprightness? Renounce God and die!" (Job 2:9).

Job answered with great wisdom: "You speak as one of the impious and foolish women would speak. What? Shall we accept [only] good at the hand of God and shall we not accept [also] misfortune and what is of a bad nature?" (v. 10). Job understood that a righteous life doesn't mean that everything always runs smoothly and that only blessings will ever fall on top of blessings.

We have two positive options open to us, and most of us can practice the first, but not all of us can accept the second. The first is to praise God *in spite of* what's going on in our lives. Or another way to say that is in the midst of our troubles and hardships, we can rejoice over the things that are not wrong in our lives. It may take effort, but if we can turn our eyes away from the immediate problems, we can see that everything in life isn't bad. We also can rejoice because God has faithfully taken us through the turmoil of the past, and we can rejoice and know that He'll do the same thing again.

The second option is to ask, "God, what can I learn from this? What do You want to teach me through this so that I may be closer to You and rejoice more fully in Your goodness?" That's not an easy question, and the answers are often even harder.

Sometimes we only grasp the important lessons in our lives when we fall flat on our faces. It's as if we're running as fast as we can and God trips us. The psalmist says: "Before I was afflicted I went astray, but now Your word do I keep [hearing, receiving, loving, and obeying it]" (Psalm 119:67). It's not that God is out to hurt us, but God loves us enough to stop us, to give us the opportunity to change our ways, and to follow Him.

Throughout my many years in ministry, I've heard stories from people who had wonderful jobs or great ministries or made a great deal of money—and then their lives fell apart. One man—someone who had once been a millionaire—came to our meetings after he had spent three years in prison. The first words that came out of his mouth were, "I'm glad I was convicted and sent to prison. I had run from God for a long time. The Lord finally got my attention when someone gave me a copy of Joyce Meyer's book *Healing the Brokenhearted.*"

Not everyone can rejoice and give thanks for their suffering, but we can all give thanks in the midst of it.

———————

God, I'm thankful for Your love and Your presence.
Forgive me for grumbling when things go wrong, and
remind me of how many things go right in my life.
Enable me to rejoice in You always. Amen.

89

Tips for Being Thankful

I will bless the Lord at all times; His praise shall continually be in my mouth. . . . Many evils confront the [consistently] righteous, but the Lord delivers him out of them all.
—Psalm 34:1, 19

All of us know we need to be thankful. God tells us to do so, and we also know from our own experience that once we seriously start praising God, our burdens and our troubles seem to weigh less heavily on our shoulders.

That's part of the power of being thankful. As we pause to give thanks to God for what's good in our lives, we also appreciate what we have. I believe God wants us to be grateful people—people who are filled with gratitude not only toward God, but also toward other people. That's my first tip: When someone does anything nice for you, let that person know you appreciate it.

One day I was going into an office building, and a man standing nearby opened the door for me. I thanked him and smiled.

"You're the fifth person I've held the door for," he said, "and you're the first one to smile and the second to thank me."

I thanked him a second time. Afterward, I thought how much we take others for granted, even when they do such simple things as open a door for a stranger.

Instead of accepting that that's the way things are, we can develop a thankful mind. Did your bus arrive on time today? If so, did you thank the driver? When you ate at the restaurant, did you thank the waiter for filling your coffee cup a second time without being asked? I could go on and on, but that's the point I want to make: Develop an attitude of gratitude toward the people in your life.

Here's another tip: Appreciate your family members, especially the person to whom you're married. I appreciate Dave, and even though we've been married a long time, I still tell him that I appreciate him. He's patient with me and thoughtful. Just those few words of thanks are a great way to develop a thankful mind and heart.

Try this: When you express appreciation, it's good for the other person to hear the words, but also remember that it releases joy in you. You enrich both your life and another person's life, even in small ways.

Another thing you can do is meditate daily on things for which you can be thankful. I have a friend who won't get out of bed in the morning until he has thanked God for at least ten things. He counts them on his fingers, and they're small things really, such as having a reliable car to drive, being a member of an exciting Sunday school class, or just being thankful that he's healthy.

He says that at night he goes to sleep by focusing on at least three things that went well that day. He relives those three positive things. For him, it can be as simple as his supervisor telling him what a good job he did on a project, or an affirming e-mail from a friend.

Here's another tip: Be thankful for the honesty in other people. No one likes to hear negative things, but sometimes you need to hear them. Of course, they may momentarily hurt your feelings, but you still can learn and grow from the experience.

I have a friend who says, "Only two people will tell you the truth about yourself: someone who's angry at you and someone who loves you very much." God uses both types of people in our lives.

So be thankful for people who tell you the truth about yourself, even if it's not what you want to hear. When you hear the truth—especially something of which you're not aware, you can change. And after you've changed, isn't that just one more thing for which you can be thankful?

God, thank You for all the good things You send into my life. Thank You for all the terrible things You don't send into my life. Thank You for the people in my life who help me grow closer to You and become a more thankful person. I pray this through Jesus the Savior. Amen.

90

Meditate on These Things

My mouth shall praise You with joyful lips when I remember You upon my bed and meditate on You in the night watches.
—PSALM 63:5b–6

Oh, how love I Your law! It is my meditation all the day.
—PSALM 119:97

*T*ranscendental Meditation. *Yoga. New Age.* We hear these terms all the time, and they cause many Christians to avoid any reference to meditation. They're afraid of the occult or pagan worship. What they don't realize is how often the Bible urges us to meditate.

We can explain biblical meditation in a number of ways, but the one I find most helpful is to think of it as expressed in the Bible. If we read the verses above (and there are many others), we see three significant things about meditation in the Word.

First, the Scriptures refer to more than a quick reading or pausing for a few brief, reflecting thoughts. The Bible presents meditation as serious pondering. Whenever the Bible refers to meditation, it speaks to serious, committed followers. This isn't a word for quick, pick-me-up Bible verses or

Precious Promises. I'm not opposed to those, but this is a call to deeper, more serious concentration.

Second, the biblical contexts show meditation as ongoing and habitual. "It is my meditation all the day," says the verse above. In Joshua 1:8, God told Joshua to meditate on the law day and night. We get the impression that the people who spoke of meditating did so seriously and threw their minds fully into the action. Psalm 1:2 says that the godly person meditates on God's law day and night.

Third, meditation has a reward. It's not just to meditate or go through a religious ritual. In most of the biblical passages where the term occurs, the writer goes on to point out the results. Again in Joshua 1:8: ". . . For then you shall make your way prosperous, and then you shall deal wisely and have good success."

Psalm 1 describes the godly person who meditates day and night on God's law (or Word) and says, ". . . and everything he does shall prosper [and come to maturity]" (v. 3).

Despite what I've pointed out, we don't talk or teach much about meditation today. It's hard work! It demands time. Meditation also demands undivided attention.

If you want to win the battle for the mind, meditation is a powerful weapon for you to use. You must focus on portions of God's Word. You must read them, perhaps repeat them aloud, and keep them before you. Some people repeat a verse again and again until the meaning fills their mind and becomes part of their thinking. The idea is that you won't put the Word of God in practice physically until you first practice it mentally.

Meditation is a life principle because it ministers life to you, and your behavior ministers life to others through you.

I could go on and on about the subject of meditating on God's Word, because it seems there is no end to what God can show me out of one verse of Scripture. The Word of God is a treasure chest of powerful, life-giving secrets that God wants to reveal to us. I believe these truths are manifested to those who meditate on, ponder, study, think about, practice mentally, and mutter the Word of God. The Lord reveals Himself to us when we diligently meditate on His Word. Throughout the day, as you go about your daily affairs, ask the Holy Spirit to remind you of certain scriptures on which you can meditate.

You'll be amazed at how much power will be released into your life from this practice. The more you meditate on God's Word, the more you will be able to draw readily upon its strength in times of trouble.

This is how we can stay filled with the Holy Spirit—stay with the Lord through meditation and through singing and praising. As we spend time in His presence and ponder His Word, we grow, we encourage others, and we win the battles against the enemy of our minds.

———————

Holy Spirit of God, help me to spend time every day meditating on the treasures of Your Word. I thank You for showing me that as I fill my mind with pure and holy thoughts, I will become a stronger and better disciple. Amen.

91

The Blessings of Meditation

*My son, attend to my words; consent and submit to my
sayings. Let them not depart from your sight; keep them in
the center of your heart. For they are life to those who find
them, healing and health to all their flesh.*
—Proverbs 4:20–22

In these verses, the writer used the words, *attend to my words,*
which is another way of exhorting us to meditate. I love the
fact that God not only frequently tells us to meditate—to
ponder seriously—His Word, but He frequently promises results. It's as if God says, "Okay, Joyce, if you meditate, here's
what I'm going to do for you."

In this passage, the promise is life and health. Isn't that
amazing? It's even a promise that when you contemplate and
brood over the Bible, it will affect your physical body.

We've known for a long time that when we fill our minds
with healthy, positive thoughts, it affects our body and im-
proves our health. This is just another way of repeating this
truth. Or take the opposite viewpoint: Suppose we fill our
minds with negative thoughts and remind ourselves how frail
we are or how sick we were the day before. We soon become

so filled with self-pity and self-defeating thoughts that we get even sicker.

In the previous pages, I've already mentioned the idea of prosperity (see Psalm 1 and Joshua 1:8). I believe that by "prosperity," God means that we'll be enriched and prosper in every part of our lives. It's not a promise of more material wealth, but an assurance of being able to enjoy all the wonderful blessings we have.

Recently when I meditated on several passages in the Bible, I realized God was showing me that the Word has hidden treasures in it—powerful, life-giving secrets—which God wants to reveal to us. They are there for those who muse, ponder, and contemplate the Word of God.

What we often forget is that God wants our fellowship, our company, and our time with Him. If we want a deep relationship with our heavenly Father, we have to make quality time for God. I recently heard someone say, "Quality time comes out of quantity times." In other words, it's only as we spend time with God on a regular, daily basis that we have those special, life-changing moments. We can't program them to happen, but if we're there on a daily basis, God will cause some of those times to be quality times of special blessing.

D. L. Moody once said that the Bible would keep us from sin, or sin would keep us from the Bible. That's the principle here. As we concentrate on God's Word and allow it to fill our thoughts, we will push away all desire to sin or to displease God in any way. We become more deeply rooted in Him. Again, think of it in the negative. When our mind remains focused on our problems all the time, we become consumed with them. If we meditate on what's wrong with others, we see even more flaws and faults. But when we concentrate on God's Word, light comes into our souls.

I want to go back one more time to that powerful statement in Philippians 4:8. No matter which translation or paraphrase we read it in, the message is powerful and exactly what we need to do to condition our minds for victory.

Here's Eugene Peterson's paraphrase in *The Message*: "Summing it all up, friends, I'd say you'll do best by filling your minds and meditating on things true, noble, reputable, authentic, compelling, gracious—the best, not the worst; the beautiful, not the ugly; things to praise, not things to curse."

Dear Father in heaven, teach me the blessings of pondering Your Word, of filling my heart and mind with Your spiritual manna. May I grow into maturity and become more and more like Your Son, Jesus. It's in His name that I pray. Amen.

92

Anointed to Bring Deliverance

The Spirit of the Lord [is] upon Me, because He has anointed Me [the Anointed one, the Messiah] to preach the good news (the Gospel) to the poor; He has sent Me to announce release to the captives and recovery of sight to the blind, to send forth as delivered those who are oppressed [who are downtrodden, bruised, crushed, and broken down by calamity], to proclaim the accepted and acceptable year of the Lord [the day when salvation and the free favors of God profusely abound].
—LUKE 4:18–19

Almost every time I finish speaking at a meeting, people come to me with sad stories of abuse and pain. I understand and often I hurt with them. I understand because I've been there. In my book *Battlefield of the Mind,* I referred to some of that dysfunctional background.[5]

I point that out because in the past, I have used my background as an excuse for not growing, for living in defeat, and for allowing Satan to control my mind.

"What else can you expect? Look where I came from." I've heard people talk that way. Perhaps it comforts them to think that whatever their past held will determine their present and their future. They have that choice if they want to believe that lie of Satan.

"Don't you know that God loves you, and that Jesus wants to deliver you from your past?" I ask. "Don't you realize that where you were is only the starting place? You can determine where you want to go and how you live your life."

I can say those words because of my background, the truth I've found in God's Word, and the Lord's deliverance that I have experienced.

From the first public appearance of Jesus recorded in Luke's gospel, I learned something powerful and significant. Jesus went to the synagogue in His hometown of Nazareth, the leader handed Him the scroll of Isaiah, and Jesus read the words printed above. What the people there didn't understand was that what He was reading to them was describing Himself: "The Spirit of the Lord [is] upon Me . . . to announce release to the captives" (v. 18).

Isn't that what Jesus did then? Isn't that what Jesus does now? He said God had anointed Him for just that task. If that's true—and I don't doubt it for a second—do I really honor Jesus by remaining a captive? If Jesus received the anointing to deliver me, there can be only one of two possible results: He sets me free or He doesn't.

This is the battlefield of the mind, as I've been pointing out again and again. Jesus says, "He has anointed Me!" The devil asks, "Did God really anoint Jesus?"

Your deliverance (and mine) depends on which voice we listen to. If we listen to Jesus and believe Him, He says that deliverance is not only possible but it is a reality. If God anointed Jesus for that purpose, it means God empowered Him. Jesus came to open prison doors and set the captives free. You and I can't be set free until we start to believe it's possible. If you believe that God loves you, wants only the best for you, and has a perfect plan for your life, how can you doubt?

You may have had a terrible, sad, and abusive past, as I did. Thousands of others have worse childhoods than you had, but they received healing. The fourth chapter of Luke tells of another synagogue where Jesus went and "... there was a man who was possessed by the foul spirit of a demon" (4:33). Jesus set him free. Jesus did that because that's what the Lord does—He sets the prisoners free, and He'll also set you free.

Lord Jesus, You have been anointed to set me free. Forgive me for listening to Satan's voice that makes me feel I'm beyond help. You are the Deliverer. In Your holy name, I ask You to deliver me from everything that holds me back from fully and totally serving You. Amen.

93

Eyes to See, Ears to Hear

*But rather what we are setting forth is a wisdom of God once
hidden [from the human understanding] and now revealed
to us by God . . . None of the rulers of this age or world
perceived and recognized and understood this, for if they had,
they would never have crucified the Lord of glory. But, on the
contrary, as the Scripture says, What eye has not seen and
ear has not heard and has not entered into the heart of man,
[all that] God has prepared (made and keeps ready) for those
who love Him [who hold Him in affectionate reverence,
promptly obeying Him and gratefully recognizing the benefits
He has bestowed]. Yet to us God has unveiled and revealed
them by and through His Spirit.*

—1 Corinthians 2:7–10

One thing used to puzzle me very much about the children
of Israel. They saw the miracles Moses performed. They witnessed the ten plagues that destroyed crops, animals, and
firstborn sons and yet never touched any of them in the land
of Goshen. They stood at the Red Sea and watched the waters
part, and later looked back to see the Egyptians drown. They
experienced miracle after miracle for forty years.

I used to ask: *Why didn't they believe?* They personally

watched signs and miracles take place, but they remained unbelievers. Except for Joshua and Caleb, every adult who watched God at work in Egypt died before the waters parted at the River Jordan.

One day as I read this passage, the answer became obvious. We don't understand God through natural eyes or human reasoning. We understand God *only when we're aided by the Holy Spirit.* Those Israelites in the wilderness *saw* miracles, but they never *experienced* God. They saw the miracles at work, but they never grasped God Himself.

That's the message Paul presents to us. He says God has prepared us—those who believe and obey—and He "unveiled and revealed" (v. 10) spiritual realities through the Holy Spirit. Another way to say this is that as long as we look only at events and facts but see nothing behind them, we don't have eyes to see and ears to hear.

That's where Satan works best. He tries to keep us blind and deaf so that we don't recognize the Spirit of God at work. For example, in a worship service, someone prays for a woman who is in great pain and she's healed. Those with eyes to see and ears to hear, immediately praise the Lord. Those who are still held by the devil's cunning lies say, "Oh, it was all psychosomatic. There was nothing really wrong with her."

I learned long ago that it did no good to argue with the spiritually blind and try to convince them to see God at work. Until the Holy Spirit enlightens them, they can never grasp the power of God at work in human lives. Only those who have been enlightened by the power of the Holy Spirit can truly grasp spiritual realities. To those who love Him and believe, God reveals spiritual truths. He assures those who have understanding that the Holy Spirit is at work. As the Spirit works in us, we gain power over every trick of the devil to blind us again.

God, enlighten me in every way. Enable me to see You in every area of my life and to rejoice in Your loving assurance and presence. I ask this in the name of Jesus Christ. Amen.

94

What's the Problem?

*All the Israelites grumbled and deplored their situation,
accusing Moses and Aaron, to whom the whole congregation
said, Would that we had died in Egypt! Or that we had died
in this wilderness! Why does the Lord bring us to this land to
fall by the sword? Our wives and little ones will be a prey. Is
it not better for us to return to Egypt?*

—NUMBERS 14:2–3

"What is your problem?" That's the question I would have
liked to ask the Israelites! Their chief occupation seemed to
be to grumble. As the verses above tell us, they not only
lamented and groaned about their situation, but they also accused Moses of bringing them into the wilderness so they
could die. In other scripture passages, we read that they complained about the food. God provided manna for them, and
all they had to do was pick it up fresh every morning—but
they didn't like the heavenly diet.

In short, it wouldn't have mattered what God did for
them or what Moses and Aaron told them. They were committed to complaining. They had formed the grumbling habit.
And much of it is a habit! If you grumble about one thing, it's
not long before there is something else to complain about.

When two moaners come together, the situation gets worse. What about the million or more people who came out of Egypt? Once the disease of disgruntlement struck, it became like a virus and infected them all. They were negative about everything. When the slightest problem arose, they were ready to return to Egypt. They preferred bondage as slaves rather than pressing on into the Promised Land.

One time Moses sent twelve spies into the land, and they came back and reported what wonderful, fertile land they had seen. (Read the story in Numbers 13 and 14.) The complainers joined with ten of the spies (again, all but Joshua and Caleb). "Yes, it's a great place," they agreed. But grumblers never stop with positive statements. They added, "But the people who dwell there are strong . . . and we were in our own sight as grasshoppers" (13:28, 33).

Had they forgotten all the miracles God had done for them? Yes, they had. That's where Satan trips up many people. They whine—and often it's about a small thing. They find fault with something. If they don't realize what they're doing by allowing such thinking to continue, they don't need to ask, "What is the problem?" What they need to learn to say is, "I don't have a problem; I am the problem."

That was exactly the situation in Moses' day. The enemy in Canaan wasn't any worse, bigger, or more powerful than what the people constantly faced. But what if their problems really were more serious? If God could destroy the Egyptians at the Red Sea, why wouldn't He give them another miracle? They were His people, and He loved them.

They themselves were the problem, and they never accepted that fact. Forty years of wandering, and they never got the message. *How dense could they be?* I've wondered many times. Of course, it's easy to say that—because I wasn't there and I can see the situation with hindsight. It's harder to examine our own lives and see why we gripe and moan.

"But my situation is different," people often say to me.

That's true, but the spirit in which you operate is the same as those in ancient Israel. You're so caught up in grumbling, complaining, and seeing what's wrong that you have no energy or time to appreciate what's good.

"What is good about your life?" I once challenged a woman who complained about almost everything.

She stared at me and realized I was serious. "Well, I have a good husband. I have two children whom I love, and they love me."

I smiled and said, "Go on."

She caught on, and her face lost its down-at-the-mouth look. Although she didn't say it in those words, she admitted, "I guess I don't have a problem. I've been the problem."

Exactly!

Spirit of God, please forgive me for seeing others or my surroundings or the situation I'm in as the problem. I've been unhappy because I haven't faced that I am my biggest hindrance to deliverance and victory. Forgive me and set me free, I pray in the name of the Savior. Amen.

95

Bad Input Produces Bad Results

Now there was no water for the congregation, and they
assembled together against Moses and Aaron. And the people
contended with Moses, and said, Would that we had died
when our brethren died [in the plague] before the Lord! And
why have you brought up the congregation of the Lord into
this wilderness, that we should die here, we and our livestock?

—NUMBERS 20:2–4

After I wrote out the verses above, I paused and read them three times. I find it difficult to believe what those people said: "Would that we had died when our brethren died [in the plague] before the Lord!" How could they have said such a terrible thing? Were they actually saying that they would rather suffer, be in torment, and die in slavery than to live freely and with God?

God's Word doesn't lie, so we must accept that those are the things they said. This passage tells me how bad their situation had become. They hadn't changed, and they wouldn't change. They wanted everything to work out for them—that is, to work out in the way they wanted it to—but they were willing to do nothing but gripe and groan.

It's the old idea that people do bad things and expect good results. They grumble at God and expect divine blessings. How can that be? How can they be so confused and twisted in their thinking? But then, I know people like that today.

Rose married an alcoholic named John, and when he got into his drunken rages, he beat her. She left, took their children, and divorced him. Two years later, Rose married again. She married John again—oh, not *that* John. The second husband's name was Ralph. He was a drunkard, and she repeated the same sad and abusive story. Her third *John* was named Ken. Although their names were different, it was as if she had married the same man (the same kind of man) three times.

When I met Rose, she grumbled and asked, "Are there any good men out there?" Of course, she later admitted that she had never attended any Christian gatherings, so she had never met a good Christian man. She only met men at parties, and she had always been attracted to man that liked to party.

My point is that it's easy to condemn the Israelites because the Bible lays out their story so clearly. Paul wrote about the wilderness wanderings and urged his readers not to ". . . discontentedly complain as some of them did—and were put out of the way entirely by the destroyer (death). Now these things befell them by way of a figure [as an example and warning to us]; they were written to admonish and fit us for right action by good instruction, we in whose days the ages have reached their climax (their consummation and concluding period)" (1 Corinthians 10:10–11).

Those stories were written to "admonish and fit us for right action by good instruction," Paul wrote. As long as you continue to act as the Israelites did in their grumbling, you'll get the same results. As long as you live like Rose, you'll have the same disastrous effect. Although I gave the example of Rose, such repetitive situations abound in any area of life. Perhaps you're someone who has your paycheck spent before you cash it. Do you dishonor God by your bad eating habits? Regardless of your situation, as long as you continue with bad inputs, you will end up with bad outcomes.

When you're tired of getting the same negative results—when you're tired of Satan buffeting you and tormenting you—then you're ready to make changes. Those people in the wilderness died outside the Promised Land because they never learned. You have an advantage: You know about them, and you also know that the Holy Spirit wants to change you.

You *can* change. You can begin by asking God to help you think positive thoughts, because positive thinking produces positive attitudes. Once your attitude changes, your life changes. It's not easy, but it is simple.

Loving Holy Spirit, please help me to think healthy, positive, and godly thoughts. Enable me to produce a good attitude that will please You and lead me into a full and lasting victory. I ask this through Jesus Christ. Amen.

96

Responsibility?

What do you think? There was a man who had two sons. He came to the first and said, Son, go and work today in the vineyard. And he answered, I will not; but afterward he changed his mind and went. Then the man came to the second and said the same [thing]. And he replied, I will [go], sir; but he did not go. Which of the two did the will of the father? They replied, The first one. Jesus said to them, Truly I tell you, the tax collectors and the harlots will get into the kingdom of heaven before you.

—Matthew 21:28–31

The story is simple. A father asks his two sons to work in his vineyard. One said no, but later changed his mind and went to work; the other said yes, but never did go into the vineyard. Jesus asked his listeners, "Which one did the will of the father?" The answer is obvious.

This story has several lessons, but one of them is about responsibility. The Father asked both sons to do the same thing. One said yes but did not fulfill what he promised. I see that kind of activity today. God constantly calls people to service, but not everyone goes. The second son is like those who get excited and tell everyone about the great call of God on their lives. But troubles come along, finances hang them up, and health problems drag them down—in short, they find many ways to avoid their responsibility to respond to God's call.

Some of us are like the son who initially refused: We resist at first, because we feel unworthy, uneducated, or unequal to the task. But eventually we surrender and do exactly what God wants.

"Which of the two did the will of the father?" Jesus asked, and everyone could see it was the reluctant one. Perhaps he counted the cost, or perhaps he wanted to be sure he could be faithful. But whatever the reason for his initial refusal, he finally said yes. He was responsible.

Let's look at the son who quickly said yes but failed to do what his father asked. I've met many people like this. When they answer the call, they're enthusiastic. They're positive this is God prompting them (and that is not for me to judge). But then God doesn't send them out immediately or things don't happen as they expect, so they encounter delays. They wait. After a while, they become impatient.

That's the crucial period where responsibility counts most: Being true to God's will when nothing seems to be happening. This is once again where you will find yourself when you fight the battle for the mind. Satan steps aside during the excitement and the glory of the call. He waits until you've started to question, *Did I hear God right? Does God really want me to do that?*

Unlike the son who held back, struggled first, and then

said yes, you've already said yes and now you're fighting to finish what you've committed yourself to do.

Responsibility is our response to God's ability. If you are going to be responsible, you must respond to the opportunities that God places in front of you. And being responsible means staying at it. It often means waiting patiently. Be like Abraham—even though he had to wait a quarter of a century for the fulfillment, God did exactly what He promised.

Young Joseph, in the Bible, had dreams that his father and brothers would bow down to him. Instead of their bowing, they threw him into a pit and sold him into slavery. But he remained faithful. He was seventeen when they sold him into slavery; he was thirty when he sold them grain. Joseph faced his responsibility—he refused to honor the negative circumstances, and he refused to listen to the devil's doubts. He held to his commitment to God.

Thirteen years may seem like a long time . . . or even thirteen days! But it's not the length of time that God counts: It's your response to His guidance. If God speaks, your responsibility is to shut your ears to doubts and open them only to God.

Heavenly Father, please forgive me for not always being responsive to You and to Your ability. Help me to focus not on circumstances and hindrances but on Your love and abundant resources. I ask this through the name of Your totally obedient Son. Amen.

97

Timing Is Everything

He who observes the wind [and waits for all conditions to be favorable] will not sow, and he who regards the clouds will not reap.

—ECCLESIASTES 11:4

Timing truly is everything. In 1984, I began Joyce Meyer Ministries. I labored faithfully and did what I believed God wanted me to do. I had a sense that God had bigger things for me, but for nine years, nothing happened to move me into those "bigger things."

In 1993, the opportunity came for Dave and me to take Joyce Meyer Ministries onto television. That was exciting, but it was also frightening. If I had given in to my old way of thinking—the negative voices that once filled my mind—I would never have moved forward. I sensed that it was a now-or-never time with God.

As Dave and I prayed, God spoke to me and said He was the One who was opening the door for me. *If you don't take the opportunity now, it will never pass your way again.* That same day Dave and I said yes.

Did the hindrances disappear? They did not. In fact, only

after we said yes did we realize what a great responsibility we had taken on. For several days, every kind of problem hit my mind as if to taunt me and say, *You're going to fall flat on your face.*

I didn't listen to those voices—as powerful as they were. I *knew* God's will. I was going to do what the Lord told me to do—regardless of the results.

I share this story with you for two reasons. First, the writer of Ecclesiastes made the same point in a different way. He wrote that if we wait for perfect conditions, we'll never do anything. We can always find reasons not to obey God.

In fact, sometimes when we say yes to God, the enemy attacks with power to make us change our minds, to arouse doubt and confusion, and to make us wonder, *Did God really call me?*

The second reason involves timing. When God says "Now!" that's exactly what God means. There's a powerful story in the Old Testament that illustrates this. Moses sent twelve spies into Canaan. Ten of the spies saw only obstacles, and the people didn't want to go into the land. God became angry, and Moses pleaded for Him to forgive the people. He did, but He still said that none of them would go into the land. Instead, all would die in the wilderness. "Moses told [the Lord's] words to all the Israelites, and [they] mourned greatly" (Numbers 14:39).

That's not the end of the incident. Early the next morning, the Israelites " . . . went up to the top of the mountain, saying, Behold, we are here, and we intend to go up to the place which the Lord has promised, for we have sinned" (v. 40).

It was too late. The Lord had given them a chance, and they had turned Him down. It was no longer the right time.

Moses asked, ". . . Why now do you transgress the command of the Lord . . . ? Go not up, for the Lord is not among you . . . For the Amalekites and the Canaanites are there before you, and you shall fall by the sword. Because you have turned away from following after the Lord, therefore the Lord will not be with you" (vs. 41–43).

That still wasn't enough for them. They went anyway, intending to take over the land—the very land God had urged them to take in His time, but not in theirs. Here's how the story ends: "Then the Amalekites came down and the Canaanites who dwelt in that hill country and smote the Israelites and beat them back, even as far as Hormah" (v. 45).

It's all in God's timing. God never says to you or to me, *Here's what I want. Do it when you're ready.* Part of listening to the guidance of the Holy Spirit is hearing the call to act when God wants you to act. The timing is everything, because it's God's timing that matters—not yours.

———————

God, it's so easy to miss Your will by not saying yes at the right time. Through Jesus Christ, I ask You to help me so that I'll be quick to hear Your voice and just as quick to obey. Amen.

98

Instant Gratification

So be patient, brethren, [as you wait] till the coming of the Lord. See how the farmer waits expectantly for the precious harvest from the land. [See how] he keeps up his patient [vigil] over it until it receives the early and late rains.

—James 5:7

"Instant gratification takes too long," my friend said and laughed. She was standing in front of the microwave. She had set the timer for ninety seconds to heat her coffee. Her toe tapped as she impatiently waited.

I smiled as I watched, but then I realized that we've been spoiled by the word *instant* in our lives today. We have instant credit approval, instant oatmeal, and instant love. We've tried to trap God into the same way of thinking. "God, give it to me now," we pray. Or if we don't use those words, that's what we mean.

One of the things I've learned from my years of Bible study is that we can't hurry the Lord. He does things in His time. In earlier meditations, I've already pointed out the long waits Abraham and Joseph completed. Moses fled into the wilderness after killing a man, and waited forty years for God to tap him on the shoulder. Rachel prayed for years to have a child, and so did Hannah, before God answered them.

When God sent Ananias to pray for the blinded Saul (later called Paul), the Lord said, ". . . Go, for this man is a chosen instrument of Mine to bear My name before the Gentiles and kings and the descendants of Israel" (Acts 9:15). After being healed, did Paul immediately rush out and preach to royalty? Years passed before God fulfilled that promise. No instant gratification there.

Many people grow impatient in waiting, and of course, the devil uses that to sneer and say, "God isn't going to do what He promised. If He were going to do it, He would have done it by now."

As I've thought about the matter of human impatience, I've realized that impatience is the fruit of pride. The proud can't seem to wait for anything with a proper attitude. It's as if they cry out, "I deserve it—and I deserve it *right now.*"

I want to point out two things from the words of James 5:7. First, God doesn't say, "Be patient *if* you wait," but "Be patient *as* you wait." He uses the beautiful example of farmers. They prepare the soil and plant the crops, and then comes the waiting. They know that in God's time, the crops will produce, and they also realize that it's a different growing season for tomatoes than it is for wheat.

Second, we need to enjoy our lives now—right now while we wait. So many people complain about wasting time (which is how they talk about waiting). Instead of pacing and grumbling about how long we have to wait in line at the grocery store or the traffic congestion on the expressway, what if you said, "Thanks, God. I can slow down now. I can enjoy this moment. Every second of my life doesn't have to be productive or bring results."

The psalmist said it this way: "My times are in Your hands; deliver me from the hands of my foes and those who pursue me and persecute me" (Psalm 31:15). This was the prayer by a man in a desperate situation. His enemies were out to kill him. Still, he didn't panic, but said, "My times are in Your hands."

Isn't that how God wants you to live? Your life and your times are in God's hands. Doesn't it follow then, that if you're facing delays and have to wait, God knows? He's the One who controls the clock of life. "My times are in Your hands." That's the way God wants you to live—and to enjoy the waiting time. Don't focus just on receiving or moving on. Focus on relishing the moments that God has given you to relax, and enjoy them as a gift from God Himself.

———————

God, I get impatient, and I want instant answers to prayers and solutions to my problems. But that's not Your way. My times are in Your hands. In the name of Jesus Christ, help me to enjoy the waiting time and remind myself that I'm waiting for You—and the wait is always worth it. Amen.

99

Too Hard?

And the Lord your God will make you abundantly prosperous in every work of your hand. . . . If you obey the voice of the Lord your God, to keep His commandments and His statutes which are written in this Book of the Law, and if you turn to the Lord your God with all your [mind and] heart and with all your being. For this commandment which I command you this day is not too difficult for you, nor is it far off. . . . But the word is very near you, in your mouth and in your mind and in your heart, so that you can do it.
—Deuteronomy 30:9–11, 14

Please make everything easy and simple for me, dear God. I don't like to struggle, and I want constant victory without exerting any effort. Let me go on my way as I let You do everything to keep me secure.

I've never heard anyone pray those words, but I have heard people pray in such a way that they were asking for an easy time in life. Too many people want victory without battle, triumph without effort, and ease without labor. God's world simply doesn't function that way.

"It's just too hard." I wonder how many times I've heard

people talk that way. I wonder how many times Joyce Meyer has talked that way. *And I did.* There was a time when I'd make a firm stand for following the Lord, but in my heart (and often in my mouth) were the words that "it was just so hard."

God convicted me of negative thinking. He taught me that if I would stop looking at the hardships and obey Him, He would make a way for me. The previous verses tell us that God wants to bless us and prosper the work of our hands, but we must obey His commandments. And in verse 11, He assures us that we can do it: "For this commandment which I command you this day is not too difficult for you, nor is it far off."

Because we spend so much time listening to the negatives and figuring out what can go wrong, too often we forget the promise that His will is not too difficult for us. Instead, it may help if you think of the obvious difficulties as blessings from God.

For instance, take encouragement from Joseph. After he spent years in Egypt and saved the lives of his family in Canaan, his brothers were afraid of him. They had hated him, plotted to kill him, and sold him into slavery. After their father, Jacob, died, they expected Joseph to punish them. He could have done that and groaned about his hard life—and his life had not been easy. Not only was he sold as a slave by his brothers, but he had been wrongly imprisoned and could have been put to death if God hadn't been with him.

Instead of saying, "Life is so hard," Joseph said, "As for you, you thought evil against me, but God meant it for good, to bring about that many people should be kept alive, as they are this day" (Genesis 50:20). He understood how God works in human lives.

Joseph didn't look at the hardships; he looked at the opportunities. Joseph didn't listen to the whispering campaign of his enemy; he turned his ears to the encouraging words of his God. In no place do we read of him complaining. He saw everything that happened to him as God's loving hand upon him.

I wrote the words *loving hand* even though it may not always seem that way. And that's where the devil sometimes creeps in to say, "If God loves you so much, why are you in this mess?"

The best answer I can give is to repeat the words of Paul the great apostle: "Let us exult and triumph in our troubles and rejoice in our sufferings, knowing that pressure and affliction and hardship produce patient and unswerving endurance. And endurance (fortitude) develops maturity of character (approved faith and tried integrity). And character [of this sort] produces [the habit of] joyful and confident hope of eternal salvation. Such hope never disappoints or deludes or shames us, for God's love has been poured out in our hearts through the Holy Spirit Who has been given to us" (Romans 5:3–5).

God never promises an easy life, but He does promise a blessed life.

God of love and compassion, please forgive me for complaining about life being too hard. Forgive me for wanting things to be easy. Lead me wherever You want me to go and, in the name of Jesus, I plead that You will help me rejoice all the way—even in the midst of the problems, because You will be there to help me solve them. Amen.

100

Truth in the Inner Being

Have mercy upon me, O God, according to Your steadfast love; according to the multitude of Your tender mercy and loving-kindness blot out my transgressions. Wash me thoroughly [and repeatedly] from my iniquity and guilt and cleanse me and make me wholly pure from my sin! For I am conscious of my transgressions and I acknowledge them; my sin is ever before me. Against You, You only, have I sinned and done that which is evil in Your sight, so that You are justified in Your sentence and faultless in Your judgment. Behold, I was brought forth in [a state of] iniquity; my mother was sinful who conceived me [and I too am sinful]. Behold, You desire truth in the inner being; make me therefore to know wisdom in my inmost heart.

—PSALM 51:1–6

The heading under this psalm reads: "A Psalm of David; when Nathan the prophet came to him after he had sinned with Bathsheba." David cried out for mercy because he had sinned with Bathsheba, and when he learned she was pregnant, he had had her husband murdered in battle.

After David confessed his sin, Nathan said to him, "The Lord also has put away your sin; you shall not die. Nevertheless, because by this deed you have utterly scorned the Lord and given great occasion to the enemies of the Lord to blaspheme, the child that is born to you shall surely die" (2 Samuel 12:13–14).

That's the first lesson I want you to grasp from this incident. When you fail God, you harm yourself, but you also bring dishonor to His name. Whenever you take a false step, there are those who watch and gleefully point their fingers. The two always go together. Not only do you bring disgrace on the name of the Lord, but you fail yourself. You knew the right but chose the wrong.

As if that were not enough, the evil one also whispers, "See how bad you are. God won't forgive you. It's too awful." Of course, he's lying, because that's what he does best. Don't listen to those words, because there is no sin you've committed that God won't forgive. You may have to carry scars or pay the penalty, but God wipes away the sin.

There's something else to learn from this: You need to face reality. You sinned. You disobeyed God. What will you do about your sin? You can plead excuses (and most of us are good at that), or you can follow David's example. When the prophet said, "You are the man . . ." (2 Samuel 12:7), the king did not deny his wrongdoing or try to justify his actions. David admitted he had sinned and confessed.

He wrote in the psalm quoted earlier: "For I am conscious of my transgressions and I acknowledge them; my sin is ever before me. Against You, You only, have I sinned and done that which is evil in Your sight, so that You are justified in Your sentence and faultless in Your judgment" (vs. 3–4).

If you follow Jesus Christ, not only are you declaring to yourself, to your family, and to the world your trust in the Savior, but you are also declaring your stand for truth. It's easy for us to deceive ourselves, but God has called us to be totally, completely, and scrupulously honest in our inner being. Don't look at what others may get away with or how they justify their behavior. We can't blame others, the devil, or circumstances.

When you fail, remind yourself that the greatest king of Israel cried out to God and said, "My sin is ever before me" (v. 3). Those sins, failures, or shortcomings (or whatever you may choose to call them) will always be there until you admit them and confess them to the Lord; only then can you know the joy of living with integrity and in truth.

This is the message for you from this final meditation; this is the message of the entire book: Strive to live with truth in your inner being. You—you and God—are the only ones who know what's in your heart. Live in honesty and truth.

Holy God, David prayed, "You desire truth in the inner being; make me therefore to know wisdom in my inmost heart." Through Jesus Christ, I plead with You to help me desire truth in my inner being, to live in such a way that I'm as honest and as open with You as I can become. I know that the life You honor is the life You bless. Amen.

NOTES

[1] Joyce Meyer, *Battlefield of the Mind* (New York: Warner Books, Inc., 1995), 40.

[2] Ibid., 128.

[3] "Count Your Blessings." Words by *Johnson Oatman, Jr.*; music by Edwin O. Excell. Included in Edwin Excell's *Songs for Young People* (Chicago: E.O. Excell, 1897).

[4] Meyer, 150.

[5] Meyer, 191–192.

ABOUT THE AUTHOR

JOYCE MEYER has been teaching the Word of God since 1976 and in full-time ministry since 1980. She is the best-selling author of more than seventy inspirational books, including *Approval Addiction, In Pursuit of Peace, How to Hear from God,* and *Battlefield of the Mind.* She has also released thousands of teaching cassettes and a complete video library. Joyce's *Enjoying Everyday Life* radio and television programs are broadcast around the world, and she travels extensively conducting conferences. Joyce and her husband, Dave, are the parents of four grown children and make their home in St. Louis, Missouri.

To contact the author, please write:

Joyce Meyer Ministries
P.O. Box 655
Fenton, Missouri 63026
or call: (636) 349-0303
Internet Address: www.joycemeyer.org

*Please include your testimony or help received from this book
when you write. Your prayer requests are welcome.*

To contact the author in Canada, please write:
Joyce Meyer Ministries—Canada
Lambeth Box 1300
London, ON N6P 1T5
or call: (636) 349-0303

In Australia, please write:
Joyce Meyer Ministries—Australia
Locked Bag 77
Mansfield Delivery Centre
Queensland 4122
or call: 07 3349 1200

In England, please write:
Joyce Meyer Ministries
P.O. Box 1549
Windsor
SL4 1GT
or call: (0) 1753-831102

OTHER BOOKS BY JOYCE MEYER

Ending Your Day Right

In Pursuit of Peace

The Secret Power of Speaking God's Word

Seven Things That Steal Your Joy

Starting Your Day Right

Beauty for Ashes Revised Edition

How to Hear From God

How to Hear From God Study Guide

Knowing God Intimately

The Power of Forgiveness

The Power of Determination

The Power of Being Positive

The Secrets of Spiritual Power

The Battle Belongs to the Lord

Secrets to Exceptional Living

Eight Ways to Keep the Devil Under Your Feet

Teenagers Are People Too!

Filled with the Spirit

Celebration of Simplicity

The Joy of Believing Prayer

Never Lose Heart

Being the Person God Made You to Be

A Leader in the Making

"Good Morning, This Is God!" Gift Book

Jesus—Name Above All Names

"Good Morning, This Is God!" Daily Calendar

Making Marriage Work (Previously
Published as Help Me—I'm Married!)
Reduce Me to Love
Be Healed in Jesus' Name
How to Succeed at Being Yourself
Eat and Stay Thin
Weary Warriors, Fainting Saints
Life in the Word Journal
Be Anxious For Nothing
Be Anxious For Nothing Study Guide
Straight Talk Omnibus
Straight Talk On Loneliness
Straight Talk On Fear
Straight Talk On Insecurity
Straight Talk On Discouragement
Straight Talk On Depression
Straight Talk On Stress
Straight Talk On Worry
Don't Dread
Managing Your Emotions
Healing the Brokenhearted
Me and My Big Mouth!
Me and My Big Mouth! Study Guide
Prepare To Prosper
Do It Afraid!
Expect a Move of God in Your Life . . . Suddenly!
Enjoying Where You Are on the Way to Where You Are
Going

The Most Important Decision You Will Ever Make
When, God, When?
Why, God, Why?
The Word, The Name, The Blood
Battlefield of the Mind
Battlefield of the Mind Study Guide
Tell Them I Love Them
Peace
The Root of Rejection
If Not for the Grace of God
If Not for the Grace of God Study Guide

JOYCE MEYER SPANISH TITLES

Las Siete Cosas Que Te Roban El Gozo (Seven Things That Steal Your Joy)
Empezando Tu Día Bien (Starting Your Day Right)

BOOKS BY DAVE MEYER

Life Lines

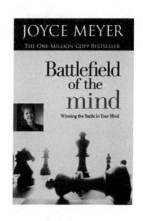
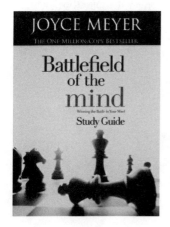